◆ Jesus

Jesus vs. Paul   59
  ◆ What Would Jesus Say?

The Wages Of Sin   68
  ◆ What Is Sin?

Can You Lose Your Salvation?   71
  ◆ I Change Not
  ◆ Sealed
  ◆ The unforgiven Servant
  ◆ The Qualifications
  ◆ Can You Undo What Jesus Did?
  ◆ The First Thing
  ◆ The Second Thing
  ◆ Blot Your Name Out Of The Book
  ◆ Can you Sin After You've Been Born Again?
  ◆ Could Jesus Have Sinned?

Grace Is Not Cheap   93

The Law Written In Their Heart & Mind   95

Willful, Intentional, Habitual Sin   97
  ◆ All Men Sin
  ◆ Unintentional vs. Intentional Sin
  ◆ Deliberate Presumptuous Sin
  ◆ No Condemnation

Be Converted   102

Grace To Serve   104

Can You Get More Grace?   105
  ◆ As You Decrease He Increases

God Hates Sin   107

God Pleasers   110

Grace In The Last Days   111

- Don't Listen To Them
- What Has Happened To My Church?
- Strong Delusion

Why Will People Go To Hell   119

Repent!   125

Confess Your Sins   128

What Grace Is Not   130

Prayers For Grace   134

Contact Info   136

NOTES   137

There's A
GRACE
For That

E. I. OSBORNE, JR.

Copyright August 2018

Deliverance Revival Tabernacle Publishing

INDEX

Introduction   5

What Is GRACE?   7
  ◆ Devine Enablement
  ◆ Grace Defined

Jesus Is Not Grace   12

Grace Imparted   15

Greater Works   16

Manifold Grace   18

There's A Grace For That   22
  ◆Grace Makes All Things Possible
  ◆ Grace Is Sufficient
  ◆ Great Grace

Grace Teaches   29

Grace Reigns   31

You Don't Have To Fall   35

Holiness & Grace   38

God Is Holy   44

We Are The Righteousness Of God   46

Sin Consciousness   47

Grace, The Law & The Ten Commandments   51
  ◆ Grace To Keep The Commandments

The Prodigal Son   56
  ◆ Adam

INTRODUCTION

This book is a comprehensive study on the grace of God, and it's affect on sin. The Lord instructed me to write this book, so that the revelations He imparted to me can be shared with the entire Body of Christ and not just the people I minister to here in New England. As you read this book, you will notice that I present a different perspective on grace than what is most commonly taught and believed.

This book was written in love and obedience, and is in no way intended to harm or discredit anyone or their ministry.

I read a statement online in a ministry e-newsletter that said; *"when people understand grace, they are empowered to change."* That statement was one of the confirmations as to why God wanted me to write this book: so that people will understand grace and be empowered to change.

If you're like me you are probably thinking; **here we go again, another book on grace**. Well, if that's the case, then let me assure you, this is far from just another book on grace. This book contains several powerful revelations on grace that I'm sure you have never heard before. I pray that by the time you finish reading this book you'll agree that it was far more than just another book on grace, and as a result of that, you will also have a desire to share it with everyone you know.

The grace of God has become somewhat of a controversial subject nowadays. That's why it has to be talked about, even if it means being criticized, or possibly offending your members and partners.

Recently, I heard several teachings on grace that I totally agreed with and some that I didn't agree with at all. There have even been some teachings on grace that I did not like, because they had a tendency to be somewhat misleading in the way they were presented. When something is taught, but people misunderstand and think you are teaching something entirely different, that's confusion. I was in a church service, and the preacher made an interesting comment about some of the teachings on grace that he heard. He said, **"I know what you're trying to say, but that's not how the people are receiving it."** What you say and what people think you said can be a world apart, and that's dangerous. Misconceptions of grace can cause people to become vulnerable to satan's ruthless plans, or even worse, it could cause them to spend eternity in hell. That's why I feel this book and its message are so important, and why it is imperative that it be shared with the entire Body of Christ.

In this book I also tackle the doctrine of whether or not you can "Lose Your Salvation." I believe this is an extremely important subject. It's the one subject that we can't afford to get wrong.

I've always believed that grace is amazing, but after seeking God and writing this book, I have an even better understanding of what grace really is and all that grace actually does. I realize now that I was clueless as to just how amazing the grace of God really is!

As a result of some of the erroneous teachings on grace, a lot of believers are depending on grace to keep them saved while they continue to sin. I on the other hand depend on grace to keep me from sinning, because that's what grace actually does.

As you read this book you will notice that I used a lot of scriptures and different Bible Translations. This was done to confirm and establish all of the points of view that I share, and to keep you from having to search for the scriptures and their different translations. In many cases I also used original Greek and Hebrew words and their definitions. It is my prayer and sincere hope that you will enjoy this book. If you do, I say, TO GOD BE ALL THE GLORY!

WHAT IS GRACE?

The dictionary defines grace as: a manifestation of favor, especially by a superior: mercy; clemency; pardon: to favor or honor. It also defines grace as: the influence or Spirit of God operating in humans to regenerate, or strengthen them.
Easton's Bible Dictionary defines grace: Favour, kindness, friendship: God's forgiving mercy: Gifts freely bestowed by God. The most commonly used definition of grace in the Body of Christ is; God's unmerited, unearned, underserved favor. This definition is most commonly used in connection with how we receive salvation, become born again, or have our sins forgiven.

If we were to take a closer look at this most commonly used definition, we would see that if we removed the adjectives unmerited, unearned, and undeserved, then all we would be left with is the word favor. So, ultimately, what we are saying is that grace is favor.
The words unmerited, unearned and undeserved are just adjectives that describe how that favor received. I believe there are different manifestations of grace. Some manifestations of grace are unmerited, unearned, and undeserved and some are not. We'll talk more about the different manifestations of grace later in the book, so please don't toss it into the fireplace just yet.

If I said, grace is favor that is unearned, unmerited and undeserved, I would still be giving an accurate definition of grace, but in a different order. When defining the grace given to receive salvation, I believe it is of utmost importance to emphasize that it is unmerited, unearned and undeserved, because that's what sets it apart and distinguishes it from favor that may have been earned, deserved, or merited. So if grace is favor that is unmerited, unearned, and undeserved, then the next question would have to be; what is favor? Favor that is unmerited, unearned, and undeserved is defined: to be divinely enabled with an ability to do something that you would otherwise be unable to do on your own. It is to be enabled to accomplish something that you would not be able to accomplish with just your natural ability. Dictionary.com defines favor as: something done or granted out of goodwill, rather than from justice or for remuneration: excessive kindness or unfair partiality; preferential treatment: to prefer; treat with partiality. So then based on everything you've just read, I think I could safely say that grace is an unmerited, unearned, undeserved divine enablement (favor) that you receive as a gift from God. (Selah)

While the Greek and Hebrew words translated favor in scripture include these definitions, there is an even deeper dimension to the Greek word for favor, *charis*. The word *charis* is translated grace almost everywhere in the New Testament. Grace denotes something given as a gift. Grace gives us special access, and positions us to receive something as a gift. I heard a pastor on television say that grace was, "divine favor, influence, and ability."

In Luke 1:28-30 Gabriel appeared to Mary and said, *"Hail, thou that art highly favoured, the Lord is with thee: blessed art thou among women. And when she saw him, she was troubled at his saying, and cast in her mind what manner of salutation this should be. And the angel said unto her, Fear not, Mary: for thou hast found favour with God."*

The scripture says Mary was highly *favoured*, and that she had found *favour* with God. The word *favoured* in verse 28 is translated from the Greek word charitoo which means; *to make graceful: to peruse with grace, compass with favor: to honor with blessings*. The word *favour* in verse 30 is translated from the Greek word charis which means: *what is due to grace*. So Mary was *favoured* (compassed with favor, honor and blessing), and as a result of that she received *favour* with God (grace or what is due to grace), to become the Mother of our Lord and Savior, Jesus Christ. The *highly favoured* status that Mary had with God might have been earned, deserved, or merited, but the *favour* that she received to conceive was unmerited, unearned, and undeserved. That *favour* (grace) was a divine enablement that caused a virgin who never knew a man to conceive and become the mother of God's only begotten Son, the Lord Jesus Christ.

I read somewhere that these two things describe what the favor of God on a person's life looks like.
1) "The favor of God can be described as tangible evidence that a person has the approval of the Lord."
2) "Favor is preferential treatment shown to somebody. It denotes acceptance, approval and pleasure."

So Mary, the mother of Jesus, was accepted and approved of by God, and as a result she received divine enablement to conceive when the Holy Ghost came upon her. Grace (unmerited, unearned, undeserved favor) enabled a virgin to conceive and have a son. Through grace, Mary was able to do something that was utterly impossible without supernatural intervention.

FAVOR THAT IS UNMERITED, UNEARNED, AND UNDESERVED IS GRACE.

I believe the term divine enablement describes what grace does. Grace divinely equips, empowers, and enables us to receive and accomplish things that would be otherwise impossible for us to have or do. Everything that we receive from God we receive by grace (unmerited, unearned, underserved favor/divine enablement), through faith. If you don't deserve salvation, can't earn it, and will never be worthy of it, then the only way that you'll ever be able to receive it is by grace. Anything you don't deserve, can't earn, and will never be worthy of, has to be given to you as a gift. That's what grace is, and that's what grace does.

This is probably a good time for me to go on record and say; **the only way to be forgiven of your sins is by grace through faith.** The "by grace" is all God's part, and the "through faith" is all our part.

DEVINE ENABLEMENT

Favor is a divine enablement. The definition of **divine** is: of or relating to a god, especially the Supreme Being: proceeding from God or a god. The definition of **enable** is; to make able: give power, means, competence, or ability to; authorize: to make possible or easy: to make ready; equip (often used in combination).
So, divine enablement is to be made able, to be authorized, or to be empowered by God. It could also mean to be made possible by God. Grace, God's unmerited, unearned, undeserved favor, divinely enables you to receive everything that you need from God. Grace divinely enables and empowers you to do things that you would otherwise be unable to do.

GRACE DEFINED

I found a lot of definitions for grace as I wrote this book, but the best one was posted on Instagram, on October 4, 2017. Not only did it define grace perfectly, but it also served as a confirmation for everything that the Lord had shown me about grace. It confirmed that what I believed about grace, and the things that I had written in this book were accurate and true.

"The word "grace" is translated from the Greek word charis, a very important word in the New Testament. But to understand what "grace" is, we must turn to its historical usage in New Testament times, because this is the background for it's use in the New Testament. Many pages could be written about the origins of the word grace, but the word charis was mostly used historically to denote a special power, even magical power, that was conveyed upon individuals by the gods or by the spirit realm. Once conferred upon a person or group of people, it imparted superhuman abilities to them. It enabled individuals to do what they could not naturally do. In some secular literature from the New Testament period, it denotes individuals who are placed under a "magic spell" that altered them, their personalities, and abilities.

When this touch of the gods or from the spirit realm, came, it always came with some type of visible manifestation. To have charis without outward evidence was simply not within the realm of possibility. Where charis was, there was always outward proof or an outward manifestation of some type. These always went hand in hand.

In the New Testament, sometimes the word charis is translated favor because it was believed that a person who received charis had been supernaturally enabled as a favor from the gods or from the spirit realm. Thus when we read of "grace" in Paul's writings, he is not only writing of a gracious act of God, but of God divinely enabling, empowering, and strengthening the recipients of it. All of this aptly depicts the word "grace" as it is used in the New Testament. This is a word coopted by the Holy Spirit from the secular world of New Testament times, and which was purified to describe what happens when the grace of God touches our lives.

Hence, when charis touched a person, it infused them and spilled over into every facet of their lives. Likewise, when the grace of God is at work in any person's life or in the life of a church congregation, it always produces a "spill over" affect with some type of outward evidence or supernatural manifestation. The grace of God, once poured out upon an individual or group of individuals, always spills over or manifests in some visible way. It's never silent or invisible. It always comes with outward demonstration.

When God's grace touches a person, it always comes to bring transformation and change. It gives the ability to repent, the ability to change, the ability to perform. It is a supernatural enabling. It results in salvation for the sinner, sanctification for the saint, and divine empowering to anyone who will yield to it."

When I read this definition it served as a confirmation for everything that the Lord had been teaching me about grace. It confirmed that what I believed about grace, and the things that I had written in this book were sound.

JESUS IS NOT GRACE

I've heard several people say that **Jesus is grace,** or **Jesus is grace personified**, but up until now I haven't been able to find any scriptural basis to confirm either of those statements. What I have found however are scriptures that say Jesus was full of grace and that grace came into the world through Jesus, but nothing that suggests that Jesus is grace or that He's grace personified.

John 1:14 says, *"And the Word was made flesh, and dwelt among us, (and we beheld his glory, the glory as of the only begotten of the Father,) full of grace and truth."*
In this verse John says that Jesus was full of grace. He does not say that Jesus is grace. Being full of something does not make you the thing. The tires on your car are filled with air, but they are not air; they're just filled with it. I can fill a cone with ice cream and then call it an ice cream cone, but the cone is not ice cream just because it's filled with it.
Luke 4:1 says, *"And Jesus being full of the Holy Ghost returned from Jordan, and was led by the Spirit into the wilderness.* Jesus was full of the Holy Ghost, so does that mean Jesus is the Holy Ghost?

John 1:16-17 says, *"And of his fulness have all we received, and grace for grace. For the law was given by Moses, but grace and truth came by Jesus Christ.* Verse sixteen tells us that we've all received of the fullness of His grace, and verse seventeen explains that this grace came by Jesus Christ. The word **came** in verse seventeen is translated from the Greek word **Ginomai.** It means: to become: to come into existence: to come to pass, happen: to appear in history, come upon stage. So grace came into existence, happened, and appeared in history through Jesus Christ. If you were asked on Sunday morning how you got to church, you might say I came by car, bus, or maybe even rickshaw, but none of those things are you. They're just the vehicle or means of transportation that you used to get you to church. Well, in the same way, Jesus was the vehicle through which grace came to New Testament believers. How did grace come? Grace came (Ginomai) by Jesus Christ.

Luke 2:40 says, *"And the child grew, and waxed strong in spirit, filled with wisdom: and the grace of God was upon him."* According to Luke, the grace of God was upon Jesus. Luke does not say that Jesus is grace. He clearly states that the grace of God was upon Him. So, John tells us that Jesus was full of grace and that grace came by Jesus, and

Luke declares that the grace of God was upon Jesus. Neither of these scriptures suggests that Jesus is grace.

John 1:1 says, *"In the beginning was the Word, and the Word was with God, and the Word was God,"* and John 1:14 says, *"And the Word was made flesh, and dwelt among us."* I do not believe that Jesus is grace, but I do believe that Jesus is the Word and the Word of God is full of grace. So based on Luke 2:40 and John 1:14 I prefer to look at it this way: Jesus, who is the Word made flesh is full of grace, and the grace of God is upon Him. The Word of God is not grace, but the grace of God is within and upon the Word.

Luke 2:52 says, *"And Jesus increased in wisdom and stature, and in favour with God and man."* Luke says that Jesus increased in *favour*. The word *favour* is translated from the Greek word *charis*, which is also translated grace in many places in the Bible. So Jesus increased in *favour* or grace with God and man during His life on the earth. If Jesus is *favour* then there's no reason for Him to increase in *favour*. I believe these scriptures confirm and establish that Jesus is not grace or a personification of grace. Yes, grace came into the world by Jesus, and grace was in and upon Him, but Jesus is not grace.

Hebrews 2:9 tells us that by the grace of God Jesus was able to taste death for every man. *"But we see Jesus, who was made a little lower than the angels for the suffering of death, crowned with glory and honour; that he by the grace of God should taste death for every man."* Jesus needed grace to suffer and die for the sins of mankind. When I think about the suffering of Jesus, it's hard for me to understand how anyone could endure that much punishment until I read this scripture that says *"that he by the grace of God should taste death for every man."* Jesus is not grace, but He definitely needed and received grace in order to fulfill His purpose of redeeming mankind.

The Bible says, *"For the law was given by Moses, but grace and truth came by Jesus Christ."* Moses and Jesus were the vessels through which the law and grace were given to mankind. The Law was given by Moses, but Moses is not the Law. Grace and truth came by Jesus, but Jesus is not grace. Jesus however is Truth, because Jesus is the Word made flesh and the Word of God is Truth.

If Jesus is grace, as some believe, and if because of grace you can't lose your salvation, then what you're saying is; Jesus gives you the ability to continue to willfully live a sin filled life after you've been born again. If that's true, then according to Galatians 2:17 (AMP), that would make Jesus an advocate or promoter of sin. *"But if, while we seek to be*

13

justified in Christ [by faith], we ourselves are found to be sinners, does that make Christ an advocate or promoter of our sin? Certainly not!" Some people have turned grace into an advocate and promoter of sin. The word advocate is translated minister in the King James Version, and it means servant.

Jesus walked in this world as a man and lived a sin-free life for thirty-three and a half years. He was able to do it, because of the Holy Ghost and the grace of God. For me, this is the proof that we can live sin free lives as well, because we have the same Holy Ghost and grace today.

I was at a minister's conference and the conference host and some of the conference speakers were complimenting each other on their ability to keep their ministries clean and free from scandal. The reason they have been able to accomplish that is, because of the Holy Ghost and grace. So, if Jesus could do it, and all of these ministers and ministries can do it, how about me, and how about you?

Hebrews 4:15 *"For we have not an high priest which cannot be touched with the feeling of our infirmities; but was in all points tempted like as we are, yet without sin."* Jesus was tempted, yet He didn't sin.
Hebrews 12:4 *"Ye have not yet resisted unto blood, striving against sin."*
1 John 2:6 *"He that saith he abideth in him ought himself also so to walk, even as he walked."*
The Bible teaches just as much about not yielding to temptation and being victorious over sin as it does about grace. I guess it all depends on where you choose to place your emphasis.

GRACE IMPARTED

According to Hebrews 10:29 in the Amplified Version, grace is imparted by the Holy Spirit. *"How much worse (sterner and heavier) punishment do you suppose he will be judged to deserve who has spurned and [thus] trampled underfoot the Son of God, and who has considered the covenant blood by which he was consecrated common and unhallowed, thus profaning it and insulting and outraging the [Holy] Spirit [Who imparts] grace (the unmerited favor and blessing of God)?"* The Holy Ghost imparts grace to us just as He imparted it to Jesus so that He could endure the shame and suffering of our redemption on the cross.

The word impartation means; to give or bestow (something, esp. an abstract quality): "to give a part of (one's possessions). The Holy Spirit is called the Spirit of grace in Hebrews 10:29 (KJV). It's The Holy Spirit that draws us to God, and then gives us an impartation of grace so that we can be forgiven of or sins, receive the salvation that Jesus purchased for us, and overcome temptation and sin. *"Of how much sorer punishment, suppose ye, shall he be thought worthy, who hath trodden under foot the Son of God, and hath counted the blood of the covenant, wherewith he was sanctified, an unholy thing, and hath done despite unto the <u>Spirit of grace</u>?"*

Hebrews 2:9 *"But we see Jesus, who was made a little lower than the angels for the suffering of death, crowned with glory and honour; that he by the grace of God should taste death for every man."* It was because of the grace of God that Jesus came and paid the price for our sins, and it was an impartation of the grace of God upon Jesus that enabled Him to endure the punishment, pain, and shame.

1 Peter 5:10 (Amp), *"And after you have suffered a little while, the God of all grace [Who imparts all blessing and favor], Who has called you to His [own] eternal glory in Christ Jesus, will Himself complete and make you what you ought to be, establish and ground you securely, and strengthen, and settle you."* The Amplified Version says that the God of all grace imparts all blessing and favor. Well, that favor is grace.

Favor (divine enablement) is an impartation of God's Power that you receive as a result of your obedience or sacrifice for the Kingdom of God. Grace (unmerited, unearned, undeserved favor) is an impartation of God's divine ability that you receive as a gift for the purpose of enabling you to do something that you are unable to do or accomplish without it.

Grace is not an impartation of Jesus; grace is an unmerited, unearned, undeserved impartation of God's divine ability.

GREATER WORKS

John 14:12 says, *"Verily, verily, I say unto you, He that believeth on me, the works that I do shall he do also; and greater works than these shall he do; because I go unto my Father."* Jesus said if we believe on him we would do the works that He did and greater works than these.

I believe the works and greater works than these should also include **BEING IN ALL POINTS TEMPTED, YET WITHOUT SIN!** Why have we limited the works and greater works than these to just healing, miracles, and the number of people we're able to reach with the Gospel of Jesus Christ? Yes, Jesus healed the sick and raised the dead, but He was also tempted in all points, yet without sin.

Hebrews 4:15 says *"For we have not an high priest which cannot be touched with the feeling of our infirmities; but was in all points tempted like as we are, yet without sin."* Jesus was tempted in all of the same ways we're tempted, yet He never gave in to the temptations and sinned. I believe it was the grace of God that enabled Him to do that, and since we have an impartation of that same grace, we can do the same thing. We can be tempted and yet not give in to the temptation, and sin. The same grace, producing the same results.

Jesus healed the sick, raised the dead, cast out devils, and multiplied fish and loaves, but we shouldn't limit the works and greater works that Jesus spoke of to just those things. I think we need to also include His compassion, His love, His anointing to teach, and His ability to resist sin as well. According to Jesus, we shall do ALL of the works that He did, and greater.

Jesus said we would do greater works, *"because I go unto my Father."* What that means is:

1) He's going to be glorified again with the glory that He once had with the Father. John 17:5 *"And now, O Father, glorify thou me with thine own self with the glory which I had with thee before the world was."*
2) We're going to receive the promise of the Spirit. Galatians 3:13-14 *"Christ hath redeemed us from the curse of the law, being made a curse for us: for it is written, Cursed is every one that hangeth on a tree: That the blessing of Abraham might come on the Gentiles through Jesus Christ; that we might receive the promise of the Spirit through faith."*
3) He defeated Satan and took back the authority that he stole from Adam and gave it to us. Luke 10:19 *"Behold, I give unto you power to tread on serpents and scorpions, and over all the power of the enemy: and nothing shall by any means hurt you."*
4) Jesus said when the Spirit of Truth is come, He shall no longer just be with us, but He's going to be in us. John 14:17 *"Even the Spirit of truth; whom the world cannot receive, because it seeth him not, neither knoweth him: but ye know him; for he dwelleth with you, and shall be in you."*

So Jesus has been glorified and given a name that is above all names. We now have authority over the devil that we didn't have before, and we have the Holy Spirit dwelling inside of us. All of that allows us to overcome all the wiles and temptations of the enemy, and God promised that He would never allow us to be tempted beyond our ability to bear it. 1 Corinthians 10:13 *"There hath no temptation taken you but such as is common to man: but God is faithful, who will not suffer you to be tempted above that ye are able; but will with the temptation also make a way to escape, that ye may be able to bear it."*

1 John 4:4 says, *"Ye are of God, little children, and have overcome them: because greater is he that is in you, than he that is in the world."* The Greater One is living on the inside of us, and because greater is in us, greater flows out of us.

Ephesians 6:11 *"Put on the whole armour of God, that ye may be able to stand against the wiles of the devil."* Grace, the Word of God, the name of Jesus, the Holy Spirit, and the anointing enable us to overcome all the wiles of the devil.

1 John 2:1 says *"My little children, these things write I unto you, that ye sin not. And if any man sin, we have an advocate with the Father, Jesus Christ the righteous."*

John says he's writing to us so that we sin not. He says *"if any man sin, we have an advocate with the Father, Jesus Christ the righteous."* John said **'IF'** any man sin, not when. If is translated from the Greek word ean which means: if or in case. I don't think it was ever believed or intended that men would continue to willfully practice sin after their salvation and conversion.

The grace of God enables us to do the works that Jesus did and greater. I believe that even includes our ability to be tempted and not sin.

MANIFOLD GRACE

Early in the book I used the term Manifold Grace and said we'd talk more about it later. Well, this is later.

What is manifold grace? Manifold Grace is a term taken from 1 Peter 4:10 that says, *"As every man hath received the gift, even so minister the same one to another, as good stewards of the manifold grace of God."*
The word **manifold** is translated from the Greek word Poikilos, and is defined as; a various colours, variegated: of various sorts; of uncertain derivation; motley that is various in character: diverse.
The dictionary defines it as; of many kinds: numerous and varied: having numerous different parts, elements, features, etc.

The term Manifold Grace is translated several different ways depending on which translation of the Bible you happen to be reading. In the King James Version the Greek words Poikilos Charis are translated *manifold grace.* The World English Translation calls it *the grace of God in its various forms.* The Bible in Basic English calls it *the unmeasured grace of God*. The Amplified Version calls it *God's many-sided grace*, and in the New International Version it's called *God's grace in its various forms.*

The idea is that grace takes on whatever form or size it needs, along with whatever attributes and characteristics necessary for the task at hand. Manifold Grace means that grace comes in diverse forms, sizes, shapes, and characteristics, for the purpose of enabling us to do something that would otherwise be impossible for us to do or accomplish on our own.

One of the reasons there's been such a raging debate about grace is, because we've limited and defined grace as the means through which we receive salvation, and we haven't understood that although grace may be the only way to receive salvation there are also other manifestations of grace that are given for various tasks and situations. The common fundamental truth about grace is that it's unmerited, unearned, and undeserved: and that only describes how grace is imparted when we need salvation. There are however manifestations of grace for every problem or situation that we may ever face. There are manifestations of grace for salvation, healing, deliverance, prosperity, and overcoming just to name a few. The Biblical term Manifold Grace suggests that there are many-many manifestations of grace, and although I can't name them all, what I can say is; there's a grace for anything and everything that you may ever need help to accomplish.

For Jesus, manifold grace is what gave Him the strength to be scourged and crucified; tasting death for all mankind. For Paul, grace was the ability to overcome his past and run the race that was set before him. It also gave Paul the strength to overcome his thorn in the flesh. 2 Corinthians 12:9 says, *"And he said unto me, My grace is sufficient for thee: for my strength is made perfect in weakness,"* and Philippians 4:13 says, *"I can do all things through Christ which strengtheneth me."* In both of these verses Paul is attributing his accomplishments to the strength of God, which was a manifestation of God's grace.

1 Corinthians 15:10 *"But by the grace of God I am what I am: and his grace which was bestowed upon me was not in vain; but I laboured more abundantly than they all: yet not I, but the grace of God which was with me."* Paul was testifying that it was only by the grace of God that he became an apostle and wrote most of the New Testament. Paul credits the grace of God laboring with him for his success.

David was given grace to defeat Goliath, and Gideon received grace to be a mighty man of valor. Samson's grace won him his greatest victory at his death, and Joseph's grace sustained him for thirteen years while in slavery and prison. The grace imparted to Moses protected him from the decree of Pharaoh to kill all the male babies. It also protected him in the ark built by his mother, and while being raised in the house of his enemy. Moses also received grace to stand fearlessly before Pharaoh and bring deliverance to the Children of Israel.

As for me, I can testify that the manifold grace of God took me from a shy, bashful young man (whose knees shook whenever he had to speak in public), and turned me into an anointed Spirit filled man (whose knees still shake a little sometimes), who declares the

19

uncompromised Word of God with confidence and boldness. I, like Paul can say; *"But by the grace of God I am what I am."*

Ephesians 2:8 says *"For by grace are ye saved through faith; and that not of yourselves: it is the gift of God."* This is a manifestation of God's grace that enables us to be saved. It is by this grace (unmerited, unearned, undeserved favor), and through our faith that we are saved. Salvation comes by grace, and by grace alone!

I believe I could say, for by grace are ye healed, for by grace are you delivered, for by grace are you helped, or even for by grace are you made whole. Everything that we receive from God is received by grace through faith. You'll never be worthy, deserving, or able to earn healing, deliverance or even help from God, so it all has to come through grace.

The grace to receive salvation is only one of the many manifestations of grace that are available to us today. Whatever your problem or situation, God has a manifestation of His grace that will empower and equip you to conquer, overcome, and be victorious over it.

Most Christians know that we can only be saved by grace, but we don't have that same awareness when it comes to receiving other things from God. For example, Paul wrote that it was *"but by the grace of God I am what I am."* In another place Paul told how he besought the Lord thrice for his thorn in the flesh and was told, *"My grace was sufficient for thee."* These are manifestations of grace that enabled Paul to fulfill his purpose and overcome any opposition. If I were to label these manifestations of grace I would call them Achieving Grace and Sufficient Grace. Without the grace of God it would have been impossible for Paul to accomplish the things that he did.

Every Child of God has or will experience these and other manifestations of God's grace at some time in their lives. In most cases these manifestations of grace are given without the person ever asking, and they may not even recognize that they've received it until after they've accomplish the task and reflect on what they did.

Philippians 4:13 says; *"I can do all things through Christ which strengtheneth me."* The strength to do ALL THINGS comes from a manifestation of the Manifold Grace of God! Whatever your problem, test, or trial, there's a manifestation of God's grace for it. There's a grace to pastor, and a grace to be an evangelist. There's a grace to preach, and a grace to teach. There's a grace to be a husband and a grace to be a wife, and there's also a manifestation of grace to be a good parent.

Have you ever heard someone say or testify, that it was only by the grace of God that they made it through a situation, succeeded, or even lived? They may have said something like; it's only by the grace of God that I'm here today, or if it had not been for the grace of God we wouldn't have made it. Statements like these and others are all testifying to the manifold grace of God. When someone says, but by the grace of God, or it was only by the grace of God, they're actually testifying about a manifestation of the manifold grace of God that equipped, empowered, and enabled them to do something impossible. Anything that you believe to be impossible becomes possible by the grace of God.

Everyday, God gives me the grace to accomplish everything that I need to accomplish that day. Whether it's grace to overcome discouragement, or grace to not burn my breakfast, it's all done by and through the Manifold Grace of God.

THERE'S A GRACE FOR THAT

The title of this book, "There's A Grace For That" is actually a description of what this book and grace are all about. For every problem or struggle you face, God has an impartation of grace that will empower you to overcome it. Whenever you're faced with a problem in life, your simple prayer should always be; Lord, give me the grace to make it through.

"There's A Grace For That" simply means, there's a manifestation of God's infinite grace that will enable you to accomplish any task, overcome any adversity, and be victorious, even in the face of insurmountable odds.

It means that grace will take on whatever form, characteristics, attributes, and size necessary to equip you to do whatever it is you need to do. No matter what the situation, the grace of God will empower and enable you to fix it, change it, or get through it every time

As it says in 1 Peter 4:10 (WEB), "***As each has received a gift, employ it in serving one another, as good managers of the grace of God in its various forms.***"

Every Sunday, God gives me the grace to minister to His people. That grace is different from the grace that He gives me to be a husband to my wife. God gives me the grace to be a pastor, but that grace is different to the grace that he gives me to be a father to my child. God gives us the grace to manage our businesses and work responsibilities, which is different from the grace that God gives us to manage our homes and family affairs. All in all, whatever it takes to achieve it, God will give you the grace to get it done; so just receive it. I'm convinced that we receive manifestations of the grace of God a lot more often than we realize. The truth of the matter is; If God hadn't bestowed a manifestation of His grace upon you, you probably wouldn't have made it this far.

There's grace to be saved, and grace to overcome (anger, drugs, the flesh, alcohol, addiction, etc.). There's grace to get out of debt, and grace to succeed. There's grace to be patient and grace to be kind, and if you're trying to lose weight, there's a grace for that as well (thank God!). Whatever you're trying to do or need to accomplish, there's a manifestation of grace that will enable you to do it.

According to Hebrews 2:9, Jesus received an impartation of the grace of God that enabled Him to suffer and *"taste death for every man."* In Genesis 39:4 & 21, Joseph had grace and favor in the sight of Potiphar and the keeper of the prison. We know that it was only by the grace of God that David defeated Goliath, and it was the grace of God on Gideon and his three hundred that enabled them to defeat the Midianites.

Just like we have "Apps" for our smart phones and wireless devices that help us solve problems, God has a manifestation of grace that will empower and enable you to overcome every issue or problem that you may ever face. If there were a grace "App," it would have to be multifaceted, with the ability to accomplish an infinite number of tasks.

2 Corinthians 9:8 says *"And God is able to make all grace abound toward you; that ye, always having all sufficiency in all things, may abound to every good work."* Grace makes you sufficient in all things. God imparts an abundance of grace to you so that you'll have everything you need to accomplish all the good works that He has called you to do.

God's grace is stronger than any addiction or sin that you may ever struggle with. So pray this; Lord, give me the grace to never again!

If you are struggling with anger, there's a grace for that. If you have been hurt and you think it's impossible to forgive, there's a grace for that. If you struggle with depression or you are tormented by fear, there's a grace for that.

Maybe you are like a lot of people and you believe it's impossible to not sin. Well, there's a grace for that too. You name it, there's a grace for it!

Romans 6:16-18 says, *"Know ye not, that to whom ye yield yourselves servants to obey, his servants ye are to whom ye obey; whether of sin unto death, or of obedience unto righteousness? But God be thanked, that ye were the servants of sin, but ye have obeyed from the heart that form of doctrine which was delivered you. Being then made free from sin, ye became the servants of righteousness."*

Jesus came to set us free from the bondage of sin. God gives us grace and truth to deliver us from the slavery of sin, and it's that same grace and truth that keep us free from sin.

Some people depend on grace to keep them from losing their salvation while they sin. I depend on grace to keep me from committing sin.

GRACE MAKES ALL THINGS POSSIBLE

"I can do all things through Christ which strengtheneth me." The strength of Philippians 4:13 is a manifestation of the grace of God! The word strengtheneth is translated from the Greek word **endunamoo** which means: endue with strength: to empower: enable. So it is Christ endowing you grace or a divine enablement to do all things.

If you desire to be victorious in every area of your life, then the Manifold Grace of God is the answer, but if all you're looking for is more excuses and reasons to fail, then you already have everything you need. Grace gives you the power to overcome, succeed and conquer every habit, struggle, temptation, or problem that you'll ever face in this life.

2 Corinthians 9:8 AMP says *"And God is able to make all grace (every favor and earthly blessing) come to you in abundance, so that you may always and under all circumstances and whatever the need be self-sufficient [possessing enough to require no aid or support and furnished in abundance for every good work and charitable donation]."*

The King James translation says, "all grace," while the Amplified Translation breaks that down to mean *"every favor and earthly blessing."* I believe both of these translations are referring to the Manifold Grace of God, or the grace of God in all of its various forms, as it's translated in the World English Bible. Grace is manifested in whatever way it needs to be manifested, to do whatever it needs to do, wherever and whenever it needs to do it!

I think most people would agree that keeping the Old Testament Mosaic Law is impossible. In the New Testament however, Paul writes in Philippians 4:13 *"I can do all things through Christ which strengtheneth me."*

Question: Is keeping the law and the commandments of the Old Testament one of the things that Paul is saying Christ can strengthen us to do? If you answered no, then my next question is, why not? If *"I can do all things through Christ which strengtheneth me"* includes everything except the Law, then that statement is false, and Paul needs to revise it. If *"all things"* does not mean all things, then the grace of God is limited and we need to notify the Body of Christ to cease and desist immediately from confessing I can do ALL things through Christ that strengthens me. Instead, we should change it from all things to some things, or maybe even most things. Let's try it out. **"I can do most things through Christ which strengtheneth me."** I happen to believe all means all!

The difference between Old and New Testament believers is the grace that came by Jesus Christ. The purpose of the Law was to show them their need for a savior, because it was impossible for righteousness to be achieved through keeping the Law. So Jesus came and paid the price for sin, and now righteousness comes by grace through faith in the finished work of Jesus. I know for some that may sound too easy, so that's why you have to know that the grace of God is real, capable, and sufficient. There are many examples of God being a God of grace in the Old Testament, but grace was not a part of their covenant for righteousness and justification. Grace in the Old Testament is usually called favor.

Not only do I believe that God's grace is sufficient for my redemption and salvation, but I also believe the grace of God can enable us to keep the Law and the Commandments. And no, we wouldn't be keeping it for the purpose of achieving righteousness, but for the purpose of living lives that are pleasing in God's sight, and keeping us free from the devil having any place or foothold in our lives.

If God has called you to it, He'll give you the grace to see you through it.

GRACE IS SUFFICIENT

In 2 Corinthians 12, God told Paul *"My grace is sufficient for thee."* Grace being sufficient means, it is everything and the only thing you need to complete any task and fulfill any assignment. The word sufficient means: adequate for the purpose; enough: competent: capable: adequate enough to meet a need or purpose. The British Dictionary defines sufficient: enough to meet a need or purpose.

2 Corinthians 12:9 (AMP) says, *"**But He said to me, My grace (My favor and loving-kindness and mercy) is enough for you [sufficient against any danger and enables you to bear the trouble manfully]; for My strength and power are made perfect (fulfilled and completed) and show themselves most effective in [your] weakness. Therefore, I will all the more gladly glory in my weaknesses and infirmities, that the strength and power of Christ (the Messiah) may rest (yes, may pitch a tent over and dwell) upon me!"***

25

The Amplified Version of the Bible defines grace as God's "favor and loving-kindness and mercy." It says grace is sufficient against any danger, and it enables you to bear the trouble manfully.

The grace of God is sufficient! It is enough to meet any need and adequate to accomplish any purpose that may arise in your life. Grace is stronger than fear, addiction, lust, or any other issue that you may face. When we are at our weakest, that's when God's grace is made perfect (fulfilled and completed).

I believe the same grace and faith through which we are saved also has the ability to keep us saved. My mother used to say; "God will keep you if you want to be kept!" and I believe that's what it comes down to; wanting to be kept. We ask God to give us the grace to accomplish all types of things, but then somehow fail to get grace for where it's needed most, our flesh. I recently heard Dr. Don Colbert talking about being disciplined with the foods that we put into our body. Well, I happen to believe that grace is sufficient for that task as well. I also happen to believe that you can receive grace to overcome sin and the sin nature.

Romans 3:23 says, *"For all have sinned, and come short of the glory of God."* The key word in that verse is have. So yes, we all have sinned, but that doesn't mean we have to continue to sin. There are a lot of things that you have done, but you don't have to keep doing them, and the grace of God makes it possible to stop.

God can give you grace to not sin (if you want it), and grace to be forgiven if you do.
2 Corinthians 12:9, *"And he said unto me, My grace is sufficient for thee: for my strength is made perfect in weakness. Most gladly therefore will I rather glory in my infirmities, that the power of Christ may rest upon me."*
God's grace is sufficient. It really is all you need for every situation. That's what God was saying to Paul after he prayed for his thorn in the flesh to depart from him. God answered and said; "My grace is sufficient for thee." God was saying, my grace is more than enough, and it's all that you need! When you have grace, the thorn that buffets you doesn't have to be removed, because grace enables you to succeed in the midst of infirmities and opposition.

If you want to be a better husband, student, preacher, or athlete, the Grace of God is all you need! The grace of God gives you strength, wisdom, power, knowledge, ability, and so much more. Grace becomes whatever you need it to be, so that you can succeed in every area of your life.

1 Peter 4:10 calls it, Manifold Grace (the grace of God in its various forms)

When Paul prayed to be delivered from a thorn in the flesh, God's answer was; "My grace is sufficient for thee: for my strength is made perfect in weakness."

The word sufficient means: **enough to meet a need or purpose; adequate for the purpose; competent; capable**. So what God was saying to Paul is: My grace is adequate, competent, and capable of enabling you to overcome the thorn in your flesh. If you like Paul are struggling with an issue or affliction of some kind, just know that the same grace that God gave to Paul is available to you as well. God's grace is the wisdom, strength, or power that you need to get the victory over whatever you're facing. There's absolutely nothing that you can't do by the grace of God!

I hear people say all the time: but for the grace of God, or if it had not been for the grace of God. I've even heard people pray: Lord, give me the grace to _____. I'm convinced that most people say and pray this without really understanding the significant and accuracy of their request.

The phrase; by the grace of God, has become just a cliché for most people. We say it without really understanding the reality of what we've said. Grace empowered us. Grace protected us. Grace directed us, and grace equipped us. All that we are or ever will be is only by the grace of God!

1 Corinthians 10:13 says, *"There hath no temptation taken you but such as is common to man: but God is faithful, who will not suffer you to be tempted above that ye are able; but will with the temptation also make a way to escape, that ye may be able to bear it."* I believe your ability to overcome temptation and the way of escape are due to an impartation of the grace of God in your life. How do we endure and escape temptation? It's only by the grace of God. Whenever we're faced with a temptation, God gives us an impartation of His Manifold Grace. The Good News translation of 1 Corinthians 10:13 says, *"Every test that you have experienced is the kind that normally comes to people. But God keeps his promise, and he will not allow you to be tested beyond your power to remain firm; at the time you are put to the test, <u>he will give you the strength to endure it,</u> and so provide you with a way out."*

27

Grace: the influence or Spirit of God operating in humans to regenerate or strengthen them. This is a definition of grace that I found online, and what I think Paul was talking about in 2 Corinthians 12:9 and Philippians 4:13. He was describing the grace of God as the strength and ability to do all things. *"I can do all things through Christ which strengtheneth me."*

The grace of God gives us the strength to endure temptation. James 1:13-14 tells us that God is not the one tempting us. It says we are tempted when we are drawn away by our own lust and enticed.

James 1:13-14 says, *"Let no man say when he is tempted, I am tempted of God: for God cannot be tempted with evil, neither tempteth he any man: But every man is tempted, when he is drawn away of his own lust, and enticed."* God gives you the grace to overcome your lust, and the grace to overcome the temptation that that lust produces.

All that I am or ever will be is, because of the manifold grace of God on my life. Where and what would I be without God's Amazing Grace. Where would I be if not for your GRACE! Romans 5:1-2 *"Therefore being justified by faith, we have peace with God through our Lord Jesus Christ: By whom also we have access by faith into this grace wherein we stand, and rejoice in hope of the glory of God."* Jesus gives us access to the grace of God, so you don't ever have to struggle to do anything on your own.

GREAT GRACE

Acts 4:33-35 says, *"And with great power gave the apostles witness of the resurrection of the Lord Jesus: and great grace was upon them all."* Great Grace produces Great Power. Everything that the apostles did was done with great power, through great grace.

28

GRACE TEACHES US

Titus 2:11-14 says, *"For the grace of God that bringeth salvation hath appeared to all men, Teaching us that, denying ungodliness and worldly lusts, we should live soberly, righteously, and godly, in this present world; Looking for that blessed hope, and the glorious appearing of the great God and our Saviour Jesus Christ; Who gave himself for us, that he might redeem us from all iniquity, and purify unto himself a peculiar people, zealous of good works."*

According to Titus, grace teaches us that we should deny ungodliness and worldly lust, and that we should live soberly, righteously, and godly in this present world. Grace not only teaches this, it also empowers us to accomplish it. The grace of God teaches and empowers us to do everything that God commands us to do. We cannot be saved through works of righteousness; but our righteous works are the evidence of repentance and conversion. I believe the purifying mentioned in verse fourteen comes through the grace of God. We're purified of all unrighteousness by grace through faith, and by grace we're also empowered to remain pure.

The Amplified version puts it this way; *"For the grace of God (His unmerited favor and blessing) has come forward (appeared) for the deliverance from sin and the eternal salvation for all mankind. It has trained us to reject and renounce all ungodliness (irreligion) and worldly (passionate) desires, to live discreet (temperate, self-controlled), upright, devout (spiritually whole) lives in this present world,"* This is accomplished through repentance and conversion.

The Good News translation says it like this; *"For God has revealed his grace for the salvation of all people. That grace instructs us to give up ungodly living and worldly passions, and to live self-controlled, upright, and godly lives in this world, as we wait for the blessed Day we hope for, when the glory of our great God and Savior Jesus Christ will appear. He gave himself for us, to rescue us from all wickedness and to make us a pure people who belong to him alone and are eager to do good."* This version tells us that grace is our instructor. Grace instructs us to give up ungodly living and worldly passions, and to live self-controlled, upright, and godly lives. It's like the virgin who makes a decision to keep herself pure and wait for her groom. Grace instructs us, and then enables us to accomplish the instruction.

Hebrews 12:28 says, *"Wherefore we receiving a kingdom which cannot be moved, let us have grace, whereby we may serve God acceptably with reverence and godly fear."* Grace empowers us to serve God acceptably with reverence and godly fear. If you can serve God acceptably, then that means there's service that's unacceptable.

So grace doesn't just teach you and then leave you to work it out through your own strength and ability. Not at all!

Grace teaches you what and how, and then empowers you to accomplish what you were taught.

Titus 2:11-13 (GNT), *"For God has revealed his grace for the salvation of all people. That grace instructs us to give up ungodly living and worldly passions, and to live self-controlled, upright, and godly lives in this world, as we wait for the blessed Day we hope for, when the glory of our great God and Savior Jesus Christ will appear."*

In each of the translations that I've presented, the word grace is translated from the same Greek word used in 2 Corinthians 12:9, where God said to Paul, *"My grace is sufficient for thee: for my strength is made perfect in weakness."* You and I have the same grace that Paul received to overcome his thorn in the flesh.

Zechariah 4:6-7 says, *"Then he answered and spake unto me, saying, This is the word of the Lord unto Zerubbabel, saying, Not by might, nor by power, but by my spirit, saith the Lord of hosts. Who art thou, O great mountain? before Zerubbabel thou shalt become a plain: and he shall bring forth the headstone thereof with shoutings, crying, Grace, grace unto it."* Zerubbabel was confronted with an obstacle that he wasn't capable of moving on his own. This obstacle is referred to as a mountain in the King James Version. The Amplified Version refers to it as a mountain [of human obstacles]. God's answer to Zerubbabel was that he would not overcome it "by might, nor by power, but by my spirit. God says; *"Who art thou, O great mountain?"* As if to say; who do you think you are mountain? God says, *"before Zerubbabel thou shalt become a plain: and he shall bring forth the headstone thereof with shouting, crying, Grace, grace unto it."* Zerubbabel overcame the mountain by grace. Grace was the force that turned Zerubbabel's mountain into a plain. The Amplified version says, *"you shall become a plain,"* another translation says *"made flat."* Grace flattened Zerubbabel's mountain and turned it into a level plain. **Grace teaches us that it's all we need to overcome the impossible.**

GRACE REIGNS

Romans 5:17 (AMP) says, *"For if because of one man's trespass (lapse, offense) death reigned through that one, much more surely will those who receive [God's] overflowing grace (unmerited favor) and the free gift of righteousness [putting them into right standing with Himself] reign as kings in life through the one Man Jesus Christ (the Messiah, the Anointed One)."*
Those who receive God's overflowing grace and free gift of righteousness will reign as kings in life with the ability to be victorious over sin. Before you received God's grace and righteousness sin reigned, but now, having received God's grace, we are empowered to reign in life and be victorious over sin.

Romans 5:20-21 says, *"Moreover the law entered, that the offence might abound. But where sin abounded, grace did much more abound: That as sin hath reigned unto death, even so might grace reign through righteousness unto eternal life by Jesus Christ our Lord."*
Romans 5:20, tells us that where sin abounded (**Gr; pleonazo: to super-abound: to exist in abundance: to increace: to make to increase**), grace did much more abound **(Gr; huperperisseuo: to abound beyond measure, abound exceedingly: to overflow, to enjoy abundantly: Verb; super abound: abound much more exceeding)**. So where sin abounded grace super abounded, abounded much more exceedingly, abounded beyond measure. This super abounding grace is not for the purpose of nullifying the consequences of our sin, but rather to equip us with a power that exceedingly abounds the power that sin has over us. So, grace is not abounding to cancel out the wages of sin, but rather to equip us to reign over sin.

Romans 5:21 says, *"That as sin hath reigned unto death, even so might grace reign through righteousness unto eternal life by Jesus Christ our Lord."*
This scripture tells us that; grace reigned through righteousness unto eternal life by Jesus Christ our Lord. Sin reigning unto death means that we were being ruled by sin (disobedience, unrighteousness, transgression), which leads to death. Grace reigning through righteousness means, that we are being ruled by the grace of God, which is empowering us to overcome sin and live righteous lives. Grace empowers us to be righteous and live righteously.

31

So if you read what Paul wrote in Romans 5:21 and then read Romans 6:1-2, it makes what Paul was trying to say take on a completely different meaning to what is traditionally taught.

"What shall we say then? Shall we continue in sin, that grace may abound? God forbid. How shall we, that are dead to sin, live any longer therein?"

Paul was asking; how can we continue to sin if grace is now reigning?

Grace is reigning, so we no longer have to be the servants of sin, because the grace of God is enabling us to reign over sin.

Wherever sin abounds, grace super-abounds so that we are empowered to not sin. The greater the temptation and desire to sin, the more grace abounds to conquer that desire. Grace doesn't abound to cover your sin and remove it's consequences. Grace super-abounds for the purpose of enabling you with the ability to conquer the lustful desires and reasons to sin. Grace divinely enables you to conquer sin. It divinely enables you to do something that you could not do otherwise.

GRACE: The influence or Spirit of God operating in humans to regenerate or strengthen them. That sounds like a divine enablement. And how do you receive divine enablement: by grace (unmerited, unearned, undeserved favor) through faith. The definition of the word **influence** is; **a power or compelling force on a person that effects the actions, behavior, or opinions of others: to move or compel a person to some action**. So this definition portrays grace as God influencing us by His Spirit to do His will and keep His commandments through regenerating **(to reform, re-create, renew, or to cause to be born again spiritually)** or strengthening us. This is what Paul was describing in 2 Corinthians 12:9 when he said God told him, *"My grace is sufficient for thee: for my strength is made perfect in weakness. Most gladly therefore will I rather glory in my infirmities, that the power of Christ may rest upon me."* Grace here is described as being God's strength and the power of Christ resting upon him. The grace of God strengthened and empowered Paul to overcome his thorn in the flesh.

Sin reigned in your life until grace came. You were subject to sin, you had no control over it, and it dominated you. But now you've received an impartation of God's grace, and the grace of God is now reigning in your life. When sin reigned you were under its control, but now that grace has come you're under its influence, and it gives you the strength and power to resist sin. Sin and the sin nature are not stronger than grace! You're desire to sin is not stronger than the grace that God gives you to overcome that desire. Wherever sin is grace abounds. Abounds means: to make to increase: to do or be more. So wherever sin is grace increases, and does and becomes more to enable you to not sin.

Romans 5:17 *"For if by one man's offence death reigned by one; much more they which receive abundance of grace and of the gift of righteousness shall reign in life by one, Jesus Christ.)"* We have received an **abundance of grace.** How much grace is that? It's enough to keep you from sinning, and to enable you to reign victorious in this life through Jesus Christ. We don't just have enough grace; we have an abundance of grace. So there's no excuse at all for us to continue to willfully practice sin.

Romans 6:14, *"For sin shall not have dominion over you: for ye are not under the law, but under grace."* The grace of God is stronger than any addiction, it's stronger than your sex drive, and it's more powerful than any lust. The law is no longer your master attempting to control you.. You're now under grace, and grace empowers you! The Law had dominion, because you didn't have grace enabling you to keep it. **Grace wasn't given so that your inability to keep the law would no longer matter.** Grace came to enable you to keep the law and the commandments, not so that you could break them without consequence.

The Law is no longer influencing and controlling your behavior, grace is. I'm living under grace and I don't have to sin, because grace sustains and empowers me.

1 John 3:9-10 *"Whosoever is born of God doth not commit sin; for his seed remaineth in him: and he cannot sin, because he is born of God. In this the children of God are manifest, and the children of the devil: whosoever doeth not righteousness is not of God, neither he that loveth not his brother."*

Verse 9 doesn't say he doesn't have to sin, it says; *"he cannot sin."* The **seed** that **remaineth** in him is the Word of God, not the Holy Spirit. God's Word is seed, and as long as you're abiding in the Word, and the Word is abiding in you, you can't sin. Abiding in the Word means you're doing it. If you stop your car at red lights, then you're abiding in the traffic laws, but if you don't, you might find yourself abiding in jail.

Hebrews 10:26 (AMP) says, *"For if we go on willfully and deliberately sinning after receiving the knowledge of the truth, there no longer remains a sacrifice [to atone] for our sins [that is, no further offering to anticipate]."*

I believe sinning in the New Testament is considered something we do willfully and deliberately, because we've been given grace, and grace

33

enables us to overcome sin. So if we sin it's no longer because we don't have the ability not to.

1 Corinthians 10:13 (AMP) says, *"No temptation [regardless of its source] has overtaken or enticed you that is not common to human experience [nor is any temptation unusual or beyond human resistance]; but God is faithful [to His word--He is compassionate and trustworthy], and He will not let you be tempted beyond your ability [to resist], but along with the temptation He [has in the past and is now and] will [always] provide the way out as well, so that you will be able to endure it [without yielding, and will overcome temptation with joy]."* So God will never allow us to be tempted beyond our ability to resist and overcome. Through the grace of God we can resist, endure, and overcome any temptation, regardless of its source. I say, **God will never give you a test you can't pass.**

YOU DON'T HAVE TO FALL

Jude 1:24 says, *"Now unto him that is able to keep you from falling, and to present you faultless before the presence of his glory with exceeding joy."*

You don't have to fall! God is able to keep you from falling. If you or someone you know is always falling, it might be, because you don't understand the grace (unmerited, unearned, undeserved, divine enablement) of God. When you understand the grace of God, not only will you not fall, you won't even stumble. The word falling is translated from the Greek word **aptaistos**, it means: not stumbling, standing firm, exempt from falling: not stumbling that is (figuratively) without sin: - from falling.

1 Timothy 1:12-14, *"And I thank Christ Jesus our Lord, who hath enabled me, for that he counted me faithful, putting me into the ministry; Who was before a blasphemer, and a persecutor, and injurious: but I obtained mercy, because I did it ignorantly in unbelief. And the grace of our Lord was exceeding abundant with faith and love which is in Christ Jesus."* Paul says the grace of God was exceeding abundant. God always goes beyond!

2 Timothy 2:1, *"Thou therefore, my son, be strong in the grace that is in Christ Jesus."* There is grace in Christ Jesus who is the Word made flesh. So, there's grace in the Word.

Hebrews 4:16, *"Let us therefore come boldly unto the throne of grace, that we may obtain mercy, and find grace to help in time of need."* God gives mercy and grace to help in your time of need. God gives you grace (unmerited, unearned, undeserved favor), or a divine enablement to meet the need.

2 Corinthians 6:1 *'We then, as workers together with him, beseech you also that ye receive not the grace of God in vain.'* Grace through faith is the only way we can receive salvation, and it's also the only way to keep it. Don't receive it in vain. After you use it to get saved, keep using it to stay saved.

2 Corinthians 8:9 (AMP), *"For ye know the grace of our Lord Jesus Christ, that, though he was rich, yet for your sakes he became poor, that ye through his poverty might be rich."* The grace of the Lord

Jesus Christ caused Him to become something so that we don't have to. He became poor, so that through His poverty we can be rich, and He became sin, so that through his suffering and sacrifice we can become the righteousness of God.

Up until now we've only been taught about the grace to receive salvation. I heard a preacher define grace as; "God's ability on you." I think that's what Paul was referring to in many of his writings. Grace, God's ability on you, will keep you from falling.
Question? Is there anything that you can't do by the grace of God? No!!! As a matter of fact, God has a grace to help you to do everything and anything. Whatever the situation; There's A Grace For It.

Hosea 4:6 says *"My people are destroyed for lack of knowledge: because thou hast rejected knowledge, I will also reject thee, that thou shalt be no priest to me: seeing thou hast forgotten the law of thy God, I will also forget thy children."* The revelations that I've received about grace have caused me to believe that it's our lack of knowledge about grace that's caused us to be destroyed. Our lack of knowledge and misunderstanding of grace has left us vulnerable to our flesh, temptation, and sin.

Paul wrote a lot about grace. He wrote so much about grace, because grace is an inexhaustible subject.

Hebrews 11:7 says *"By faith Noah, being warned of God of things not seen as yet, moved with fear, prepared an ark to the saving of his house; by the which he condemned the world, and became heir of the righteousness which is by faith."* By faith Noah built the ark, and his righteousness and obedience in building the ark condemned the world of his day. Why did Noah's obedience condemn the world? Noah's obedience condemned the world, because it was the proof that men could have faith, obey God, and be righteous. His obedience testified against the disobedience of the people of his of his day. Noah's obedience said; if it's possible for one man to have faith, obey God, and live right, then it's possible for all men to have faith, obey God, and live right.

Just as Noah was the proof in his day that men could live right and obey God, Jesus is the proof in our day that men can live right and obey God. Hebrews 4:14-15 says, *"Seeing then that we have a great high priest, that is passed into the heavens, Jesus the Son of God, let us hold fast our profession. "For we have not an high priest which cannot be touched with the feeling of our infirmities; but was in all points tempted like as we are, yet without sin."* We have the same Holy Spirit and grace that Jesus had when He was tempted, yet without sin. The man Jesus testifies against all of the people who say it's impossible to not sin.

The first time I taught that You Don't Have To Fall, a friend of mine told me he always believed falling was inevitable. Romans 10:17 says, *"So then faith cometh by hearing, and hearing by the word of God."* My friend had faith in the idea that it's impossible not to fall, because that's what he had always heard. What do you think would've happened if he was hearing, you don't have to fall, because of the grace of God? I think he'd have faith to not fall. So I wrote a book and called it, **You Don't Have To Fall**.

Noah faced all of the same temptations in his day as every other man yet he did not sin. 2 Peter 2:5 calls Noah a preacher of righteousness. *"And spared not the old world, but saved Noah the eighth person, a preacher of righteousness, bringing in the flood upon the world of the ungodly"*

One translation calls Noah *"the sole voice of righteousness."* Noah was a witness and example of righteousness in his day, and Jesus is a witness and example of righteousness in our day. Jesus being tempted yet without sin is the proof that we can be tempted and not sin. Jesus is the proof that men can live right and obey God, and His witness condemns the unrighteous of today just as Noah's obedience condemned the unrighteous of his day.

Genesis 9:20-21 says, *"And Noah began to be an husbandman, and he planted a vineyard: And he drank of the wine, and was drunken; and he was uncovered within his tent."* Noah drank of the wine, became drunk as a result, and was uncovered in his tent. This happened after the waters of the flood had subsided, and some commentaries believe Noah may not have been aware of the strength and intoxicating power that the wine possessed, or it was and inadvertent act. Either way, it is not an act of unrighteousness.

Noah didn't fall, Jesus didn't fall, and you don't have to fall!

1 Corinthians 10:13 says, *"There hath no temptation taken you but such as is common to man: but God is faithful, who will not suffer you to be tempted above that ye are able; but will with the temptation also make a way to escape, that ye may be able to bear it."* God will never give you a test you can't past, or a temptation you can't resist and overcome.

HOLINESS & GRACE

1 Peter 1:13-16 (KJV) says, *"Wherefore gird up the loins of your mind, be sober, and hope to the end for the grace that is to be brought unto you at the revelation of Jesus Christ; As obedient children, not fashioning yourselves according to the former lusts in your ignorance: But as he which hath called you is holy, so be ye holy in all manner of conversation; Because it is written, Be ye holy; for I am holy."*

1 Peter 1:13-16 (NIV) says, *"Therefore, with minds that are alert and fully sober, set your hope on the grace to be brought to you when Jesus Christ is revealed at his coming. As obedient children, do not conform to the evil desires you had when you lived in ignorance. But just as he who called you is holy, so be holy in all you do; for it is written: "Be holy, because I am holy."* In this verse God is telling New Testament, New Covenant, saved by grace believers that they should be holy. The reason God can command and expect us to be holy is, because of the grace that is brought to us at the revelation of Jesus Christ. God tells us to be holy and gives us the grace (favor) to do it. This command to be holy is confirmed in Ephesians 4:22-24.

Ephesians 4:22-24 says, *"That ye put off concerning the former conversation the old man, which is corrupt according to the deceitful lusts; And be renewed in the spirit of your mind; And that ye put on the new man, which after God is created in righteousness and true holiness."* This verse is a confirmation to 1 Peter 1:13-16. Both of these verses are about repentance and grace. Putting off the former conversation the old man (your lifestyle), and renewing and girding up the spirit of your mind is repentance.

The new man is not born in sin and "shapen" in iniquity, but is created *"in righteousness and true holiness"* with the grace to live as obedient children.

The word holy is translated from the Greek word hagios, which means; most holy thing, a saint. The origin of hagios is from hagos which means; (an awful thing): sacred (physically pure, morally blameless or religious ceremonially consecrated): (most) holy (one thing) saint. So God gives us the grace to be physically pure and morally blameless, because we are ceremonially consecrated to Him.

Some people believe that holiness is an act of legalism which is no longer necessary, because we're under a covenant of grace. Well, yes, we are under a New Covenant, but God tells New Testament, New Covenant believers to be holy, and then gives us the grace to do it.

I believe the same grace that saves you also enables you to live a holy life, and without grace, neither one of these things would be possible. Grace is God's unmerited, unearned, undeserved favor. It enables you to be forgiven of your sins, and also divinely enables you to overcome the temptations and desires to sin.

God can command us to be holy, because He knows that He has given us the grace to make it possible. An impartation of the grace of God makes all things possible. Philippians 4:13 says, *"I can do all things through Christ which strengtheneth me."*

Ephesians 5:1-13 says, *"Be ye therefore followers of God, as dear children; And walk in love, as Christ also hath loved us, and hath given himself for us an offering and a sacrifice to God for a sweetsmelling savour. But fornication, and all uncleanness, or covetousness, let it not be once named among you, as becometh saints; Neither filthiness, nor foolish talking, nor jesting, which are not convenient: but rather giving of thanks. For this ye know, that no whoremonger, nor unclean person, nor covetous man, who is an idolater, hath any inheritance in the kingdom of Christ and of God. Let no man deceive you with vain words: for because of these things cometh the wrath of God upon the children of disobedience. Be not ye therefore partakers with them. For ye were sometimes darkness, but now are ye light in the Lord: walk as children of light: (For the fruit of the Spirit is in all goodness and righteousness and truth;) Proving what is acceptable unto the Lord. And have no fellowship with the unfruitful works of darkness, but rather reprove them. For it is a shame even to speak of those things which are done of them in secret. But all things that are reproved are made manifest by the light: for whatsoever doth make manifest is light."*

Verse 5 says *"For this ye know, that no whoremonger, nor unclean person, nor covetous man, who is an idolater, hath any inheritance in the kingdom of Christ and of God."* Whoremongers, the unclean, the covetous and idolaters have no inheritance in the kingdom of God. The term unclean person is taken from the Greek word akathartos which means; not cleansed: in a ceremonial sense: that which must be abstained from according to the Levitical Law: in a moral sense; unclean in thought and life. The scripture tells us very specifically that the unclean (unholy) have no inheritance in the Kingdom of Christ and of God. There are those however who would have you believe that after you're born again you can continue to be a whoremonger, an idolater, covetous, or an unclean person, because you're under grace.

Well, I wholeheartedly disagree with that, and so does the Word of God when it says; "*Be not ye therefore partakers with them."*

Ephesians 5:6-7 (AMP) says, *"Let no one deceive you with empty arguments [that encourage you to sin], for because of these things the wrath of God comes upon the sons of disobedience [those who habitually sin]. So do not participate or even associate with them [in the rebelliousness of sin]."* Verse seven calls sin an act of rebellion, and the Bible tells us where all of the rebellious will be for all eternity. It also defines the sons of disobedience as those who habitually sin. Willful, continual, habitual sin is mentioned in the New Testament along with its consequences. Some would argue that their grace message is not encouraging anyone to sin, and technically it isn't, but it definitely doesn't discourage people from sinning either. It portrays sin as something that doesn't matter.

Paul's writing's to the Ephesians about sin doesn't surprise me at all. In fact, his writings make even more sense when I consider what the Bible says in the books of Malachi and Hebrews. Malachi 3:6 says, *"For I am the Lord, I change not; therefore ye sons of Jacob are not consumed."* Hebrews 13:8 says, *"Jesus Christ the same yesterday, and to day, and for ever."* God has not, and will not change. When God made a promise to Abraham, it was His immutability that caused Abraham to be fully persuaded that God would do what He said, even though Sarah was barren, and the fact that both of them had become to old to produce children.

God has never allowed sin to be in His presence or Kimgdom and He never will. That's why God gives us grace to have our sins cleansed, and grace to resist temptation and overcome sin.

In order for God to allow sin in His Kingdom (of which born again believers are a part of), He would have to change His nature and character, and grace doesn't do that. The grace of God doesn't change His nature and character; it enables us to change ours.

2 Peter 3:9 says, *"The Lord is not slack concerning his promise, as some men count slackness; but is longsuffering to us-ward, not willing that any should perish, but that all should come to repentance."* It is not God's will that any should perish, but that all should come to repentance. The word perish is taken from the Greek word apollumi. It means: to destroy: to lose: to put out of the way entirely: to devote or give over to eternal misery in hell. God's will is that all come to repentance. The word repentance is taken from the

40

Greek word metanoia and it means: a change of mind. I believe the change of mind pertains to how we think about sin. When we consider Christ suffering and sacrifice we shouldn't want to continue to sin even if grace made it possible, but rather, we should have a desire to stop sinning, and the grace of God makes that possible.

Based on the scriptures I've just given you, I believe God wants us to repent and be holy after we're saved by grace through faith. I believe the Bible teaches that New Covenant, New Testament, saved by grace believers need to repent after they receive salvation. Repentance does not produce salvation, it's merely the renewing of the mind mention in Romans 12:1, and 2 Peter 3:9, just to name a few.

Romans 12: 2, *"And be not conformed to this world: but be ye transformed by the renewing of your mind, that ye may prove what is that good, and acceptable, and perfect, will of God."* After we're transformed spiritually by grace through faith there's a natural transformation that needs to take place as well. That happens as we renew our minds, or change the way we think.

1 Corinthians 3:16-17 says, *"Know ye not that ye are the temple of God, and that the Spirit of God dwelleth in you? If any man defile the temple of God, him shall God destroy; for the temple of God is holy, which temple ye are."*

1 Corinthians 6:19-20 says, *"What? know ye not that your body is the temple of the Holy Ghost which is in you, which ye have of God, and ye are not your own? For ye are bought with a price: therefore glorify God in your body, and in your spirit, which are God's."*
Your body is the temple of God. Do you really believe that God has given you grace so that you can defile the temple in which He dwells? The scripture tells us plainly that He will destroy those who defile His temple, whose temple ye are. I believe God gives you grace so that you can keep your body, which is His temple, holy.

1 Corinthians 6:15-18 *"Know ye not that your bodies are the members of Christ? shall I then take the members of Christ, and make them the members of an harlot? God forbid. What? know ye not that he which is joined to an harlot is one body? for two, saith he, shall be one flesh. But he that is joined unto the Lord is one spirit. Flee fornication. Every sin that a man doeth is without the body; but he that committeth fornication sinneth against his own body."*
Our bodies are members of Christ. We're joined to the Lord and we're one spirit. Therefore, we're told to flee fornication. When you join

yourself to a harlot you become one with the harlot. If God forsook Jesus when he became sin for us, I don't think He's going to dwell in a temple that's continually being defiled. The grace of God is imparted to us, so that we have the ability to overcome the lust of the flesh and keep the temple holy.

God has never tolerated willful continual sin, or allowed sin to be in His presence. His holiness won't allow it. **In order for God to tolerate sin in His presence He would have to change His nature and character.** God said I AM HOLY! And that's never going to change. He said in Malachi 3:6 *"For I am the Lord, I change not."* God has always been a God of grace. He was a God of grace before the Law and He was a God of grace while the Mosaic Law was in effect. The reason Cain, David, and Moses didn't die after they committed murder is, because of the grace and mercy of God.

1 Thessalonians 4:1-8 (AMP) says: *"**Finally, believers, we ask and admonish you in the Lord Jesus, that you follow the instruction that you received from us about how you ought to walk and please God (just as you are actually doing) and that you excel even more and more [pursuing a life of purpose and living in a way that expresses gratitude to God for your salvation]. For you know what commandments and precepts we gave you by the authority of the Lord Jesus. For this is the will of God, that you be sanctified [separated and set apart from sin]: that you abstain and back away from sexual immorality; that each of you know how to control his own body in holiness and honor [being available for God's purpose and separated from things profane], not [to be used] in lustful passion, like the Gentiles who do not know God and are ignorant of His will; and that [in this matter of sexual misconduct] no man shall transgress and defraud his brother because the Lord is the avenger in all these things, just as we have told you before and solemnly warned you. For God has not called us to impurity, but to holiness [to be dedicated, and set apart by behavior that pleases Him, whether in public or in private]. So whoever rejects and disregards this is not [merely] rejecting man but the God who gives His Holy Spirit to you [to dwell in you and empower you to overcome temptation].**"*
If I were to preach this without you seeing it written in the scripture, a lot of people would call it legalism.
1 John 3:1-10 (AMP) says, *"**See what an incredible quality of love the Father has shown to us, that we would [be permitted to] be named and called and counted the children of God! And so we are! For this reason the world does not know us, because it did not know Him.**"*

42

Beloved, we are [even here and] now children of God, and it is not yet made clear what we will be [after His coming]. We know that when He comes and is revealed, we will [as His children] be like Him, because we will see Him just as He is [in all His glory]. <u>*And everyone who has this hope [confidently placed] in Him purifies himself, just as He is pure (holy, undefiled, guiltless). Everyone who practices sin also practices lawlessness; and sin is lawlessness [ignoring God's law by action or neglect or by tolerating wrongdoing--being unrestrained by His commands and His will].*</u> *You know that He appeared [in visible form as a man] in order to take away sins; and in Him there is [absolutely] no sin [for He has neither the sin nature nor has He committed sin or acts worthy of blame].* <u>*No one who abides in Him [who remains united in fellowship with Him--deliberately, knowingly, and habitually] practices sin. No one who habitually sins has seen Him or known Him.*</u>

Little children (believers, dear ones), do not let anyone lead you astray. The one who practices righteousness [the one who strives to live a consistently honorable life--in private as well as in public-- and to conform to God's precepts] is righteous, just as He is righteous. <u>*The one who practices sin [separating himself from God, and offending Him by acts of disobedience, indifference, or rebellion] is of the devil [and takes his inner character and moral values from him, not God]; for the devil has sinned and violated God's law from the beginning.*</u> *The Son of God appeared for this purpose, to destroy the works of the devil.* <u>*No one who is born of God [deliberately, knowingly, and habitually] practices sin, because* I.e. *in human terms, God's seed is like a divine "genetic code" which is passed on to His children and produces in them the desire to live in a way which pleases Him.* *God's seed [His principle of life, the essence of His righteous character] remains [permanently] in him [who is born again--who is reborn from above--spiritually transformed, renewed, and set apart for His purpose]; and he [who is born again] cannot habitually [live a life characterized by] sin, because he is born of God and longs to please Him.*</u> *By this the children of God and the children of the devil are clearly identified:* <u>*anyone who does not practice righteousness [who does not seek God's will in thought, action, and purpose] is not of God, nor is the one who does not [unselfishly] love his [believing] brother."*</u>

No comment or explanation necessary.

GOD IS HOLY

1 Peter 1:16 *"But as he which hath called you is holy, so be ye holy in all manner of conversation; Because it is written, Be ye holy; for I am holy.* A holy God says, *"be holy for I am holy."* God will never ask you to do something that you can't do, or that He's not planning to give you the power and ability to do. The word holy is translated from the Greek word hagios. It means: most holy thing, a saint. The origin of hagios is hagos. Hagos means: sacred (physically pure morally blameless 0r religious ceremonially consecreated): (most) holy (one thing) saint. When God commands us to **be holy,** He is telling us to take on His character, and He gives us the grace to do it.

When God says, *"I am holy,"* He is describing His very nature and character. "*For I Am Holy"* tells us who and what God is.
1 John 4:8 & 16 says God is love, and in 1 John 1:5 it says God is light. So God is Love, God is Light, and God is Holy.

In order for darkness and sin to be in God's presence and kingdom He would have to change His nature. Love is God's only motivation for everything that He does, because He is Love. Darkness can't remain in God's presence, because He is Light, and sin can't be in the presence of God, because he is Holy. Grace does not change God's nature; it enables us to change ours. It is impossible for God to change His character and nature, so He gives us grace and commands us to change; "**be ye holy for I am holy.**"

Our nature is changed supernaturally when we're born again. Ephesians 4:22-24, Colossians 3:9-11, and Romans 12:2 tell us to put off the old man with his deeds which is the natural transformation.

Ephesians 4:22-24 *"That ye put off concerning the former conversation the old man, which is corrupt according to the deceitful lusts; And be renewed in the spirit of your mind; And that ye put on the new man, which after God is created in righteousness and true holiness."*

Colossians 3:9-11 *"Lie not one to another, seeing that ye have put off the old man with his deeds; And have put on the new man, which is renewed in knowledge after the image of him that created him: Where there is neither Greek nor Jew, circumcision nor uncircumcision, Barbarian, Scythian, bond nor free: but Christ is all, and in all."*

Romans 12:2 *"And be not conformed to this world: but be ye transformed by the renewing of your mind, that ye may prove what is that good, and acceptable, and perfect, will of God."*

The only way that the Gospel Of Grace message that's being taught today could be true is if God were to change His nature and character. God is, was, and always will be holy.

WE ARE THE RIGHTEOUNESS OF GOD

2 Corinthians 5:21 *"For he hath made him to be sin for us, who knew no sin; that we might be made the righteousness of God in him."*

We have been made the righteousness of God in Christ Jesus. Jesus, who knew no sin, was made sin for us; that we might be made the righteousness of God in Him. The word righteousness is translated from the Greek word dikaiosune which means; the condition acceptable to God: a state approved of God: Integrity, virtue, purity of life, rightness, correctness of thinking feeling, and acting: Justice or the virtue which gives each his due.

Jesus didn't become sin so that we could continue to willfully practice sin. We are made righteous by grace through faith, but not for the purpose of being able to sin and that sin not separate us from God. I don't believe grace makes it possible for a righteous person to willfully, continually commit fornication, adultery, lie, steal, or sow discord among the brethren. I don't believe that's what Jesus suffered and died for.

1 John 3:7-10 *"Little children, let no man deceive you: he that doeth righteousness is righteous, even as he is righteous. He that committeth sin is of the devil; for the devil sinneth from the beginning. For this purpose the Son of God was manifested, that he might destroy the works of the devil. Whosoever is born of God doth not commit sin; for his seed remaineth in him: and he cannot sin, because he is born of God. In this the children of God are manifest, and the children of the devil: whosoever doeth not righteousness is not of God, neither he that loveth not his brother."*
We are the righteousness of God in Christ Jesus. Verse 7 says *"he that doeth righteousness is righteous."* The evidence of the righteousness that we received when we were born again is in the righteousness that I do.

SIN CONSCIOUNESS

The sins that you should never be conscious of is, your past, confessed, forgiven sins. According to Isaiah 43:25, God has forgiven, forgotten, and blotted out the sins of your past. So there is absolutely no reason for you to have any awareness or consciousness of past sin. *"I, even I, am he that blotteth out thy transgressions for mine own sake, and will not remember thy sins."*

Micah 7:19 (AMP) says, *"He shall again have compassion on us; He will subdue and tread underfoot our wickedness [destroying sin's power]. Yes, You will cast all our sins Into the depths of the sea."* Your confessed, forgiven sins are GONE!

There are two types of sin consciousness. There's consciousness of past sin and consciousness of the potential of future sin. There's no reason to be conscious of past sin, because it's been blotted out and forgotten; IT'S GONE! But, if you lose the consciousness of the potential of future sin, that's dangerous. That's like forgetting about the lusts of your flesh and the snares that your adversary is constantly setting for you. 1 Peter 5:8 says, *"Be sober, be vigilant; because your adversary the devil, as a roaring lion, walketh about, seeking whom he may devour."* The word vigilant is translated from the Greek word gregoreou which means: to watch: give strict attention to, be cautious, active: to take heed lest through remission and indolence some destructive calamity suddenly overtake one: to keep awake that is watch. The opposite of consciousness is unconsciousness. We should never be in a state of unconsciousness when it comes to our adversary and his desire to devour us through sin. Sin gives place to the devil. Without it, he has no authority to devour us.

The reason Eve disobeyed God in the Garden of Eden by eating of the fruit of the tree of the knowledge of good and evil was, because Satan deceived her and she lost her sin consciousness. As long as Eve believed there would be consequences for her sin (she was sin conscious) she was safe. The moment Satan deceived her, and she believed that her sin wouldn't lead to death (spiritual & physical) she sinned. Not being sin conscious is like driving without being conscious of the speed limit, pedestrians, or traffic lights and signs.

The erroneous teachings about grace are Satan's attempt to take away your sin consciousness as he did with Eve. Once you sin and you're separated from God, Satan, the thief, can steal, kill, and destroy. I believe it's better to be sin conscious; aware of the possibility that you could sin, and aware of the grace available to you if you do. Not consciousness of past forgiven sins, but conscious of the potential of future sin. Maybe I could call it, Future Sin Consciousness.

I was required to take a defensive driver class many years ago. The purpose of the class was to increase your awareness of all the things that could potentially cause an accident. This creates more of a defensive attitude while driving, because the defensive driver is more likely to spot the possibility of an accident and avoid it. Is it better to be accident conscious; or should you just drive along unconscious of the potential dangers all around you? Consciousness of a thing puts you in a better position to avoid it.

The word conscious means: aware of what one is doing: fully aware of or sensitive to something (often followed by of). So if I take away your sin consciousness, I take away your awareness and sensitivity to what you're doing; which in this case would be sin. A person who completely loses their sensitivity and consciousness of sin might be described as being in lasciviousness.

I believe sin consciousness is having an awareness of sin and it's consequences. The false teachings on grace remove that awareness by telling you that grace has removed the consequences of sin, and if there are no consequences then there is no need to be conscious of it. That to me is a recipe for disaster.

Romans 12:1 *"I beseech you therefore, brethren, by the mercies of God, that ye present your bodies a living sacrifice, holy, acceptable unto God, which is your reasonable service."* Paul writes and beseeches (begs) us to present our bodies as living sacrifices, holy, and acceptable unto God. We are to be living sacrifices (live as a sacrifice, gift, offering, that is holy, and acceptable). Holy and acceptable means: most holy thing, a saint, sacred, physically pure morally blameless or religious ceremonially consecrated. That's what Jesus meant in Mark 8:34. *"And when he had called the people unto him with his disciples also, he said unto them, Whosoever will come after me, let him deny himself, and take up his cross, and follow me."* A living sacrifice denies himself, takes up his cross, and lives a holy acceptable life. In Matthew 10:38 Jesus said, *"And he that taketh not his cross, and followeth after me, is not worthy of me."* Jesus is speaking to future believers, because He said *"take up his cross."*

48

In order to drive a car you have to be aware or conscious of the traffic laws and rules of the road. To drive in Massachusetts where I live you start by taking a written exam and obtaining a learners permit. This allows you to drive while accompanied by a licensed adult. Studying the Massachusetts Drivers Manual and passing the learner's permit exam proves that you know the traffic laws and the basic automobile functions that will allow you to operate a motor vehicle safely. If you attempted to drive a vehicle without knowing the traffic laws and remaining conscious of them while driving, you would be putting yourself and everyone around you in grave danger.

Walking through life completely oblivious to the possibility of sinning puts you and everyone around you in danger. I think the best way to live is to be sin and grace conscious. That way, I'm aware of the possibility of sin and the grace available to me that enables me to not sin. I believe that's what grace gives us; the ability to live a holy, acceptable life. Not the ability to continue to live a life of sin while grace somehow keeps us holy.

From Genesis too Revelations God talks about sin. If He didn't want us to be sin conscious He certainly didn't show it in His Word. In Genesis 2:16-17 God said, *"And the Lord God commanded the man, saying, Of every tree of the garden thou mayest freely eat: But of the tree of the knowledge of good and evil, thou shalt not eat of it: for in the day that thou eatest thereof thou shalt surely die."* That sounds like God making Adam conscious of sin and it's consequence. In Acts 5:5-10 Ananias and his wife Sapphira dropped dead after they lied to the Holy Ghost. That story might tend to make you a little sin conscious, and Revelations 21:8 will definitely raise your consciousness of sin and it's consequences. *"But the fearful, and unbelieving, and the abominable, and murderers, and whoremongers, and sorcerers, and idolaters, and all liars, shall have their part in the lake which burneth with fire and brimstone: which is the second death."*

The only reason to not be sin conscious is if you believe that you can practice sinning without the penalty of being separated from God, which is popularly referred to as losing your salvation or eternal security.

If you're walking through the jungle, it's probably a good idea to be conscious of the different types of creatures that live there. Well, I think in the same way we should be conscious of our flesh and it's desire to commit sin. The moment we forget or take for granted the lust of the flesh, is the moment when we could potentially find

49

ourselves overcome by it. Romans 6:19-20 refers to it as the infirmity of the flesh. *"I speak after the manner of men because of the infirmity of your flesh: for as ye have yielded your members servants to uncleanness and to iniquity unto iniquity; even so now yield your members servants to righteousness unto holiness. For when ye were the servants of sin, ye were free from righteousness."*

When I got married my wife and I exchanged rings. These rings serve as a symbol of the covenant that we entered into on our wedding day. We don't have to wear them to keep us conscious of the fact that we're married, but they do make other people conscious of our marital status. I hope my wife never loses consciousness of the fact that she's married to me.

I pray that you lose all consciousness of your confessed, forgiven sin, but remain conscious of the grace of God to be forgiven of future sin, and to be enabled to not sin.

1 Corinthians 10:12 says, *"Wherefore let him that thinketh he standeth take heed lest he fall."*
(AMP) *"Therefore let the one who thinks he stands firm [immune to temptation, being overconfident and self-righteous], take care that he does not fall [into sin and condemnation]."*

I also pray that the Holy Spirit continue to convict and keep you conscious of any sin you may currently be committing, and bring you to a place of confession and repentance.

Galatians 5:19-21 has a list of what the Bible calls "the works of the flesh." As I read through them I noticed that the works of the flesh are also things that are forbidden under the Law and the commandments. The first commandment is *"Thou shalt have no other gods before me."* This is idolatry, and it's listed as one of the works of the flesh. *"Thou shalt not kill, and Thou shalt not commit adultery"* are the sixth and seventh commandments, and they're also listed as works of the flesh.

Some people believe that the Law and the Ten Commandments have no relevance or significance for New Testament believers. I believe that's only partially true. I believe the Law and Ten Commandments have no relevance or significance for New Testament believers as far as their redemption, justification, righteousness, and forgiveness of their sin is concerned, because under the New Covenant we're saved by grace through faith and not by the works of the Law.

I do however believe that the Law and Commandments have significance and still play a role in our moral behavior and lifestyle, but not for the purpose of achieving righteousness or justification. Galatians 3:11 says, *"But that no man is justified by the law in the sight of God, it is evident: for, The just shall live by faith."*

Romans 7:6 says, *"But now we are delivered from the law, that being dead wherein we were held; that we should serve in newness of spirit, and not in the oldness of the letter."* We've been delivered from the law, and the only way to receive salvation is by grace through our faith.

Hebrews 8:10 and Hebrews 10:16 tell us that God has placed His Laws in the hearts and minds of His people. Hebrews 8:10 says, *"For this is the covenant that I will make with the house of Israel after those days, saith the Lord; I will put my laws into their mind, and write them in their hearts: and I will be to them a God, and they shall be to me a people."*
Hebrews 10:16 says, *"This is the covenant that I will make with them after those days, saith the Lord, I will put my laws into their hearts, and in their minds will I write them."*
After the old covenant was abolished, God wrote His law in the hearts and minds of His people. These two verses of scripture reveal the significance of the Law and Commandments to New Testament, New

Covenant Believers. Instead of the Commandments being written on tablets of stone, God wrote them on the fleshly tablets of our hearts. God says; I will be your God, and ye shall be My people. God's people have His Law written in their hearts and minds.

If God weren't concerned about us keeping the Law and Commandments, He wouldn't have written them in such an important, significant, intimate place. The Law being in your heart and mind means that it should influence your thoughts and direct your actions. The two things that have changed about the Law and Commandments is; their purpose and location. I believe the Law and Commandments are as important today as they have always been, and maybe even more important, because of where God placed them. The difference in their purpose is they're no longer used as a way of achieving justification and righteousness; they're now only used as a source of moral guidelines for God's people to live by.

John 14:15 says, *"If ye love me, keep my commandments."* Jesus said if we love Him we'd keep His commandments. He didn't say we have to keep the commandments, He just said if we loved Him we would. In the Old Testament the Law was kept out of fear and to achieve righteousness. Under the New Covenant we keep the Commandments as an act of obedience in Love. It's all about God loving us, and our loving Him, because He first loved us.

John 15:4-5 says, *"Abide in me, and I in you. As the branch cannot bear fruit of itself, except it abide in the vine; no more can ye, except ye abide in me. I am the vine, ye are the branches: He that abideth in me, and I in him, the same bringeth forth much fruit: for without me ye can do nothing."* In verse 5 Jesus says without Him we can do nothing, and in verse 4 He says, *"Abide in me, and I in you. As the branch cannot bear fruit of itself, except it abide in the vine."* The fruit that Jesus is talking about are the fruit of the Spirit mentioned in Galatians 5:22-23. *"But the fruit of the Spirit is love, joy, peace, longsuffering, gentleness, goodness, faith, Meekness, temperance: against such there is no law."*

Without Jesus, who is the Word of God, we can't bear the fruit of Galatians 5:22-23, love, joy, peace, etc.

1 Corinthians 6:9-12 says, *"Know ye not that the unrighteous shall not inherit the kingdom of God? Be not deceived: neither fornicators, nor idolaters, nor adulterers, nor effeminate, nor abusers of themselves with mankind, Nor thieves, nor covetous, nor*

drunkards, nor revilers, nor extortioners, shall inherit the kingdom of God. And such were some of you: but ye are washed, but ye are sanctified, but ye are justified in the name of the Lord Jesus, and by the Spirit of our God. All things are lawful unto me, but all things are not expedient: all things are lawful for me, but I will not be brought under the power of any." Fornication, idolatry, adultery, etc., are all forbidden under the Old Covenant Laws and Commandments, and in the New Testament under the New Covenant, people that do these things will not inherit the Kingdom of God.

In Ecclesiastes 12:13-14 Solomon said, *"Let us hear the conclusion of the whole matter: Fear God, and keep his commandments: for this is the whole duty of man. For God shall bring every work into judgment, with every secret thing, whether it be good, or whether it be evil."*
Solomon said, the whole duty of man is to *"fear God, and keep his commandments."* This is all that God desired when He created man in the Garden of Eden, and I believe this is all God desires today. It seems to me that a lot of people have allowed grace to take away their fear (respectful reverence) of God. God didn't give us grace so that we can continue to sin and disrespect Him, but rather, God gave us grace to enable us to keep His commandments, and respectfully reverence Him in everything that we do.

GRACE TO KEEP THE COMMANDMENTS

In John 14:15 Jesus said; *"if ye love me, keep my commandments."* I don't believe Jesus was only speaking to the Jews who were still under the old covenant. I believe Jesus was and is talking to everyone that claims to love Him. The keeping of His commandments is the evidence of your love. John 14:21 says *"He that hath my commandments, and keepeth them, he it is that loveth me: and he that loveth me shall be loved of my Father, and I will love him, and will manifest myself to him."* Anyone can claim to love you, but the real proof of their love is in their actions. The reason I have complete assurance of God's love for me is, the price that He paid to redeem me. John 3:16 says, *"For God so loved the world, that he gave his only begotten Son, that whosoever believeth in him should not perish, but have everlasting life."* 1 John 3:16 says, *"Hereby perceive we the love of God, because he laid down his life for us: and we ought to lay down our lives for the brethren."* Love without works (corresponding action) is dead, just as faith without works is dead.

1 John 5:2-3, *"By this we know that we love the children of God, when we love God, and keep his commandments. For this is the love of God, that we keep his commandments: and his commandments are not grievous."*

Luke 6:46 Jesus said *"And why call ye me, Lord, Lord, and do not the things which I say?"*
In Matthew 7:21 Jesus said, *"Not every one that saith unto me, Lord, Lord, shall enter into the kingdom of heaven; but he that doeth the will of my Father which is in heaven."*
When Jesus said this, He was talking about New Covenant believers.

In the next verse Jesus said, *"Many will say to me in that day, Lord, Lord, have we not prophesied in thy name? and in thy name have cast out devils? and in thy name done many wonderful works?"* I think verse 22 confirms that Jesus was talking to born again, Spirit filled believers, because prophesying, casting out devils, and the gifts of the Spirit are all part of the New Covenant for New Testament believers. So people who are operating in the gifts of the Spirit while at the same time not doing God's Will, are workers of iniquity, and Jesus says He never knew them.

Matthew 7:24,26,27, *"Therefore whosoever heareth these sayings of mine, and doeth them, I will liken him unto a wise man, which built his house upon a rock: And the rain descended, and the floods came, and the winds blew, and beat upon that house; and it fell not: for it was founded upon a rock. And every one that heareth these sayings of mine, and doeth them not, shall be likened unto a foolish man, which built his house upon the sand: And the rain descended, and the floods came, and the winds blew, and beat upon that house; and it fell: and great was the fall of it."* Whoever is doing God's Word is wise, and whoever is not doing God's Word is foolish.

John 15:10, *"If ye keep my commandments, ye shall abide in my love; even as I have kept my Father's commandments, and abide in his love."*
2 John 1:6, *"And this is love, that we walk after his commandments. This is the commandment, That, as ye have heard from the beginning, ye should walk in it."*

Why are there so many scriptures about keeping the Commandments in the New Testament if the Commandments no longer matter? Could it be that the frequency of their appearance is an indication of how much they matter, and how important it is for us to keep them? I've often heard it said that when God repeats Himself pay attention, because whatever He's repeating must be important.

Most people would agree that the Law and the Ten Commandments were and are impossible to keep, but what if God gave you the grace to keep them? I'm not asking because it's necessary to keep them, I'm just asking is it possible if God gave you the Grace. I ask this question, because although justification doesn't come by the law, it is still important for us to be able to obey God and live a life that's pleasing in His sight.

I think people under the Old Covenant couldn't keep the law, because they didn't have grace. God knew it was impossible for them to keep the law and the commandments by their own strength, so that's why God gave us grace. The grace of God enables us to do the impossible. Grace enables you to do the impossible, and receive the unattainable.

Exodus 20:13-17, are some of the Ten Commandments. *"Thou shalt not kill. Thou shalt not commit adultery. Thou shalt not steal. Thou shalt not bear false witness against thy neighbour. Thou shalt not covet thy neighbour's house, thou shalt not covet thy neighbour's wife, nor his manservant, nor his maidservant, nor his ox, nor his ass, nor any thing that is thy neighbour's."*
These are some of the things that some people claim grace allows you to do. My question is; why would you want grace to be able do this stuff? I think that says a lot about those people.

I think the Ten Commandments are ten things that born again, Spirit filled believers shouldn't want to do.

THE PRODIGAL SON

I've heard several people say, no matter what you do or how bad you are, your father will always be your father. They use that as an example as to why your sin won't separate you from God, and why you can't lose your salvation. The idea is that when you're born again God becomes your heavenly Father, and no matter what you do that can't change. Your father is your father and nothing can change or undo that. There are three people that I'll point to in scripture that I believe have a bearing on that idea. The first one is the prodigal son, the second one is Adam, and the third would be Jesus. In all of these cases, the issue is not relationship it's fellowship.

THE PRODIGAL SON

The issue with the prodigal son is not relationship to his father it's fellowship. Your father will always be your father, but that doesn't mean you're in fellowship with him. The Prodigal son didn't lose his relationship with his father; he lost fellowship. His father was still his father, and he was still his son, but they had no fellowship. When the prodigal son returned home it was the fellowship that he had with his father that was restored not the relationship. Nowhere in the story does it suggest that he was no longer related to his father. Even after the son left, he called him his father and the father called him his son. The son said he wasn't worthy to be called his son, but the father shows us very plainly that that was never the case in his mind. He was always his son even while he was out of fellowship with him.

Even though they never lost relationship, it was the loss of fellowship that prevented the father from helping his son in any way. The son knew his father had enough bread to spare, but he was still starving, because their fellowship had been severed. The father may have even been aware of his sons condition, but he was unable to help him, because although they were related and the father still loved him, they were out of fellowship.

Luke 15:17-20, "*And when he came to himself, he said, How many hired servants of my father's have bread enough and to spare, and I perish with hunger! I will arise and go to my father, and will say unto him, Father, I have sinned against heaven, and before thee, And am no more worthy to be called thy son: make me as one of thy hired servants. And he arose, and came to his father. But when he was yet a great way off, his father saw him, and had compassion, and ran, and fell on his neck, and kissed him. And the son said unto him, Father, I have sinned against heaven, and in thy sight, and am no more worthy to be called thy son."*

The prodigal son's loss of fellowship meant that he forfeited all of the benefits of being a son. When he lost fellowship with his father he lost access to all of the provisions, pleasures and protection of his father's house. He also lost fellowship with his brother and all of his father's servants as well.

ADAM

Adam and Eve lost fellowship with God when they ate of the forbidden fruit. God was still their Father and Creator, but the fellowship was lost. They lost fellowship with God as a result of their disobedience. God had no choice but to evict them from the Garden of Eden and separate Himself from them. Adam and Eve's loss of fellowship meant that they no longer had access to the presence and blessings of God. They were expelled from the Garden of Eden, and were forced to provide for themselves through their own toil. They were separated from God, which is spiritual death, and were destined to die physically and be separated from God for all eternity in the Lake of Fire, which is the second death.

I believe the willful continual practice of sin and disobedience will still lead to separation from God, because God is a Holy God and sin cannot be in His presence.

JESUS

Matthew 27:46 says, *"And about the ninth hour Jesus cried with a loud voice, saying, Eli, Eli, lama sabachthani? that is to say, My God, my God, why hast thou forsaken me?"*
When God the Father forsook Jesus, His only begotten Son, He was still His Father. He forsook Jesus because of the sin of the world that had been placed upon Him. God was still His Father, but they were out of fellowship. When Jesus died He went into the lower parts of the earth where Hell (Hades) and Paradise were located. During that time, Jesus didn't feel God's presence, God wasn't talking to Him, and angels weren't ministering to Him, because He was in Hell where there is no fellowship. I say that Jesus was in Hell not Paradise, because He

became sin for us, and because of that He wouldn't qualify to go to Paradise. Paradise was a place for the righteous dead, and although Jesus had no sin and had done no wrong, He had our sin placed upon Him as the Lamb of God that taketh away the sins of the world. Our sin kept Him from Paradise until the full price for our sin was paid. Once that price was paid He was resurrected and lead captivity captive. John 3:14, is a type and picture of Jesus on the cross with the sins of the world on Him. Jesus became sin for us, and in that state He is portrayed as a serpent. *"And as Moses lifted up the serpent in the wilderness, even so must the Son of man be lifted up."* Our sin made Him like the serpent in the wilderness. This would have kept Him out of Paradise and sent Him to Hell until the full penalty for our sin was paid.

My dad is with the Lord in Heaven. He will always be my dad, but we've been separated by his death. We're still related and we still love each other, but we no longer have fellowship. Loss of fellowship removes all the benefits of relationship.

God created Lucifer, he chose to rebel and become Satan. His rebellion separated him from God, but that didn't change the fact that God was his creator. They have relationship, but not fellowship. Don't let the devil deceive you and rob you of your fellowship with God.

The prodigal son received grace to be reconciled to his father and have their fellowship restored. God offers sinners that same grace and reconciliation today.

JESUS vs. PAUL

Whenever I've heard people teach about grace they usually mention Paul and reference the various scriptures on grace that he wrote. The Apostle Paul wrote most of the New Testament, and he wrote more about grace than anyone else in the Bible. So it's not surprising that the majority of the grace messages are taught using his writings. One of the problems I have with this is, most teachings on grace refer to what Paul said about it, but somehow make it completely opposite to what Jesus taught about it.

One day, after seeking the Lord for clarity and understanding about grace, the Lord spoke to me and said; *if preachers are saying that what Paul said about sin and grace is different than what Jesus said about sin and grace then they're wrong.* Paul and Jesus were not saying two different things about sin and grace. So why are so many preachers claiming that they were?

One of the explanations that I've heard is, **"Jesus and Paul were speaking to different audiences."** They say that Jesus was speaking to people under the law, while Paul was speaking to people under grace. Now, as good as that may sound I can't agree with it, because that would mean that although Jesus brought grace He didn't teach grace, and that's not true. Also, Hebrews 13:8 says that Jesus Christ is the same, yesterday, and today, and forever, and Malachi 3:6 says, "For I am the LORD, I change not."

The idea of different audiences reminds me of Genesis 3:1 where Satan said, *"Now the serpent was more subtil than any beast of the field which the Lord God had made. And he said unto the woman, Yea, hath God said, Ye shall not eat of every tree of the garden?"* Satan is a subtle master of deception, and he always has an answer and reasons that will convince you that it's all right to sin. Satan would like you to believe the different audiences theory, because it helps to legitimize the erroneous teachings on grace and eternal security. Paul never taught that it was all right to sin, or that sin wouldn't separate you from God. Anyone who teaches that is doing it based on a misinterpretation of scripture, not rightly dividing the scripture correctly, or maybe due to a bogus, deceptive revelation of scripture. Whenever someone is trying to make it possible to sin without consequences that should get your attention. Many years ago I heard a preacher trying to suggest that homosexuality was all right, because God made you that way. Well, if that were the case then God wouldn't have labeled it an abomination. If Paul thought grace made it possible to sin without being separated from God, then he wouldn't have written Romans 6:23, *"For the wages of sin is death; but the gift of God is eternal life through Jesus Christ our Lord."* Sin still produces death, and God still offers the gift of salvation by grace through faith if you sin.

Jesus came teaching and preaching the Gospel, The Good News. Luke 4:18-19 says, *"The Spirit of the Lord is upon me, because he hath anointed me to preach the gospel to the poor; he hath sent me to heal the brokenhearted, to preach deliverance to the captives, and recovering of sight to the blind, to set at liberty them that are bruised, To preach the acceptable year of the Lord."* This is all about grace and freedom from the Law! The brokenhearted could be healed, the captives can be delivered, the blind can see, and the bruised can be liberated, all by grace, without the keeping of the Law. The lepers weren't healed because they kept the Law, they were healed by grace, and were told to show themselves to the priest to confirm their healing so that they could be allowed back into society.

If *"grace and truth came by Jesus Christ,"* according to John 1:17, then Jesus and Paul were preaching the same thing, but Jesus taught it first. Jesus was introducing grace to people who were under the law. Jesus didn't teach the law because the people were under the law, He taught the gospel of grace to deliver people from the law. That's why in Matthew 5:43-44 He said, *"Ye have heard that it hath been said, Thou shalt love thy neighbour, and hate thine enemy. But I say unto you, Love your enemies, bless them that curse you, do good to them that hate you, and pray for them which despitefully use you, and persecute you."* Jesus said, "ye have heard that it hath been said, but I say unto you," because He was replacing the Law (what hath been said) with grace.

If I didn't know what grace was and what grace does, then I might be able to accept the idea of Jesus and Paul preaching to two different audiences, but because I understand how grace works I realize that Jesus was teaching against sin, because He came to give them the power to overcome sin through this magnificent gift called grace.

Once you realize what grace is, then you can understand why Jesus said *"And if thy right eye offend thee, pluck it out, and cast it from thee: for it is profitable for thee that one of thy members should perish, and not that thy whole body should be cast into hell. And if thy right hand offend thee, cut it off, and cast it from thee: for it is profitable for thee that one of thy members should perish, and not that thy whole body should be cast into hell."* (Matthew 5:29-30) Jesus said if your right hand offends you cut it off. Offend here means, cause to sin.

Jesus, who grace and truth came by, never suggests that our sins will no longer separate us from God under the New Covenant of grace, because He knew that grace would deliver us from the power of sin and enable us to overcome it. Under the New Covenant, sin has lost its power and grace reigns!

Romans 5:21, *"That as sin hath reigned unto death, even so might grace reign through righteousness unto eternal life by Jesus Christ our Lord."* Grace reigns and enables us to overcome sin and live righteous. The word reign is translated from the Greek word basileuo. It means: to exercise the highest influence, to control. So sin is no longer controlling you, grace is.

Jesus said in Matthew 5:17-19, *"Think not that I am come to destroy the law, or the prophets: I am not come to destroy, but to fulfill. For verily I say unto you, Till heaven and earth pass, one jot or one tittle shall in no wise pass from the law, till all be fulfilled. Whosoever therefore shall break one of these least commandments, and shall teach men so, he shall be called the least in the kingdom of heaven: but whosoever shall do and teach them, the same shall be called great in the kingdom of heaven."*

Jesus said whosoever breaks one of the least of the commandments, and shall teach men so, he shall be called the least in the kingdom of heaven: but whosoever shall do and teach them, the same shall be called great in the kingdom of heaven. Whoever teaches that it's all right to lie, steal, or commit adultery is called the least in the kingdom, but whoever keeps the commandments and teaches others that by the grace of God they can keep them as well, is called great in the Kingdom of Heaven. This is not about the Law and legalism, it's about the power and ability of the grace of God. It's not about keeping the commandments to be righteous, it's about keeping the commandments because you want to, and by the grace of God you can.

Jesus said that those who do and teach the law shall be called great in the kingdom of heaven. He said this knowing that the grace of God would enable us to do it and keep it. Jesus did not preach the law; He preached grace. The Bible says, grace and truth came by Jesus Christ. John 1:17 says, *"For the law was given by Moses, but grace and truth came by Jesus Christ."* Grace and Truth came by Jesus preaching, teaching and demonstrating it. The leper, the centurion's servant, and the woman with the issue of blood didn't deserve to be healed, couldn't earn healing, and they would never be worthy of healing. Jesus healing them was a demonstration of grace. Jesus taught and demonstrated grace through the things that He did.

During Jesus' ministry, He was always doing things that were contrary to the law. Jesus said He came to fulfill the law, and although Jesus is the fulfillment of the law, He never encouraged anyone to not keep the law as in the case of the lepers who Jesus healed. Jesus told them to go and show themselves to the priest to fulfill the requirements of the law, and as an act of faith. Luke 17:14, *"And when he saw them, he said unto them, Go shew yourselves unto the priests. And it came to pass, that, as they went, they were cleansed."* That's healing by grace through their faith.

If Jesus were preaching and teaching the Law He would have allowed the people to stone the woman caught in adultery. John 8:3-7 says, *"And the scribes and Pharisees brought unto him a woman taken in adultery; and when they had set her in the midst, They say unto him, Master, this woman was taken in adultery, in the very act. Now Moses in the law commanded us, that such should be stoned: but what sayest thou? This they said, tempting him, that they might have to accuse him. But Jesus stooped down, and with his finger wrote on the ground, as though he heard them not. So when they continued asking him, he lifted up himself, and said unto them, He that is without sin among you, let him first cast a stone at her."* Under the Law this woman should have died, but instead she received grace.

Paul never preached that your sin wouldn't separate you from God, and neither did Jesus. Both of them were preaching and introducing grace, but grace does not give us the ability to commit sin without the consequence of being separated from God. Jesus said repent for the remission of sin, and Paul said "shall we continue to sin? God forbid!" Paul is teaching the non-continuance of sin, or repentance just as Jesus was.

Hebrews 12:4 says, *"Ye have not yet resisted unto blood, striving against sin."* I would compare what Paul said in Hebrews 12:4 to what Jesus said in Matthew 5:29-30. *"And if thy right eye offend thee, pluck it out, and cast it from thee: for it is profitable for thee that one of thy members should perish, and not that thy whole body should be cast into hell. And if thy right hand offend thee, cut it off, and cast it from thee: for it is profitable for thee that one of thy members should perish, and not that thy whole body should be cast into hell."* (Some believe the author of Hebrews is unknown)

Hebrews 12:15-17 Amplified Version, talks about us failing to secure God's grace. The Good News Translation calls it turning back from the grace of God, and the Message Translation calls it trading away God's lifelong gift in order to satisfy a short-term appetite. In Hebrews 12:16 (MSG), sinning after receiving salvation is compared to Esau selling his birthright for a piece of bread to satisfy the appetite of his flesh. The Message translation calls it Esau Syndrome, and it's amazing that so many people are suffering from that syndrome today. *"Watch out for the Esau syndrome: trading away God's lifelong gift in order to satisfy a short-term appetite."*

Mark 8:34 says, *"And when he had called the people unto him with his disciples also, he said unto them, Whosoever will come after me, let him deny himself, and take up his cross, and follow me."* Jesus said to the people and the disciples, if you're going to follow me you're going to have to deny yourself. I believe denying yourself is the real heart of the grace issue. Is it necessary or even required that you deny your flesh and sinful nature, or does grace allow you to continue to satisfy the lust of the flesh without the consequence of being separated from God? As Paul said, God forbid! That's not what grace is for!

In the next verses (Mark 8:35,36) Jesus says, *"For whosoever will save his life shall lose it; but whosoever shall lose his life for my sake and the gospel's, the same shall save it. For what shall it profit a man, if he shall gain the whole world, and lose his own soul?"* Jesus is saying, if you choose to save your life instead of denying yourself and losing it, you'll not only lose your life, but eternal life as well. You might gain the whole world, but you'll lose your soul.

Matthew 10:38 says, *"And he that taketh not his cross, and followeth after me, is not worthy of me."* When you think of what sin produced and what Jesus had to endure to atone for it; why would you want to continue to sin.

If Jesus and Paul were preaching two different messages, then that would mean that grace came by Paul's teachings, and that Jesus changed. Jesus is the Word made flesh, so the question is; is Jesus the Old Testament Word made flesh, the New Testament Word made flesh, or both? He's both, and He remains the same yesterday, and today, and forever more. Malachi 3:6 God says, *"For I am the Lord, I change not; therefore ye sons of Jacob are not consumed."* God is a HOLY God and He has never allowed sin in His Kingdom or presence, and He never will.

1 Corinthians 6:9-10, *"Know ye not that the unrighteous shall not inherit the kingdom of God? Be not deceived: neither fornicators, nor idolaters, nor adulterers, nor effeminate, nor abusers of themselves with mankind, Nor thieves, nor covetous, nor drunkards, nor revilers, nor extortioners, shall inherit the kingdom of God."*

Galatians 5:19-21, *"Now the works of the flesh are manifest, which are these; Adultery, fornication, uncleanness, lasciviousness, Idolatry, witchcraft, hatred, variance, emulations, wrath, strife, seditions, heresies, Envyings, murders, drunkenness, revellings, and such like: of the which I tell you before, as I have also told you in time past, that they which do such things shall not inherit the kingdom of God."* Jesus brought grace and Truth, but He never made a provision for sin or the works of the flesh. Jesus never suggested that it was all right to sin, or that because of grace, your sin would no longer separate you from God. Paul didn't teach that either.

Ephesians 5:5, *"For this ye know, that no whoremonger, nor unclean person, nor covetous man, who is an idolater, hath any inheritance in the kingdom of Christ and of God. Let no man deceive you with vain words: for because of these things cometh the wrath of God upon the children of disobedience. Be not ye therefore partakers with them. For ye were sometimes darkness, but now are ye light in the Lord: walk as children of light."* This is what God says to New Testament, New Covenant, saved by grace believers.

Mark 2:23-28 *"And it came to pass, that he went through the corn fields on the sabbath day; and his disciples began, as they went, to pluck the ears of corn. And the Pharisees said unto him, Behold, why do they on the sabbath day that which is not lawful? And he said unto them, Have ye never read what David did, when he had need, and was an hungred, he, and they that were with him? How he went into the house of God in the days of Abiathar the high priest, and did eat the shewbread, which is not lawful to eat but for the priests, and gave also to them which were with him? And he said unto them, The sabbath was made for man, and not man for the sabbath: Therefore the Son of man is Lord also of the sabbath."* The disciples of Jesus plucked corn on the Sabbath. Plucking the corn was work and that was breaking the Law, but Jesus didn't stop or rebuke them. This is not how someone who is preaching the Law would have responded. This is another example of Jesus introducing grace. If Jesus were preaching the law, He wouldn't have healed on the

Sabbath. If He were preaching the Law, He would have allowed the woman with the issue of blood and the woman caught in adultery to be stoned, because both of them had broken the Law.

Matthew 9:1-2 says, *"And he entered into a ship, and passed over, and came into his own city. And, behold, they brought to him a man sick of the palsy, lying on a bed: and Jesus seeing their faith said unto the sick of the palsy; Son, be of good cheer; thy sins be forgiven thee."* The scribes considered what Jesus said blaspheme. They reasoned that only God could forgive sin. Jesus used this as an opportunity to show that the Son of man had power on earth to forgive sin, and to introduce forgiveness and healing by grace through faith.

Mark 1:14-15 says, *"Now after that John was put in prison, Jesus came into Galilee, preaching the gospel of the kingdom of God, And saying, The time is fulfilled, and the kingdom of God is at hand: repent ye, and believe the gospel."* Jesus went into Galilee preaching the Gospel of the Kingdom of God, not the Law. Jesus said, repent and believe the gospel. All you have to do to receive salvation is believe the Gospel and confess it. That's grace! and that's what Jesus preached to people under the Law.

WHAT WOULD JESUS SAY? (WWJS)

What would Jesus say about sin if He were here today? Would Jesus preach about grace the same way we hear some preaching it today? Personally, I DON'T THINK SO!!! Jesus would not preach on grace as a means to continue to sin and fulfill the lust of the flesh. I think if Jesus were here preachers would be ashamed to look at His nail scared hands and feet and tell people it's all right to sin because you've got grace.

Romans 6:15-18 MSG, Paul says that just because we're under grace, and we're free from the "tyranny" of the old covenant does not mean we can do anything we want.

Romans 6:15-18 (MSG), *"So, since we're out from under the old tyranny, does that mean we can live any old way we want? Since we're free in the freedom of God, can we do anything that comes to mind? Hardly. You know well enough from your own experience that there are some acts of so-called freedom that destroy freedom. Offer yourselves to sin, for instance, and it's your last free act. But offer yourselves to the ways of God and the freedom never quits. All your lives you've let sin tell you what to do. But thank God you've started listening to a new master, one whose commands set you free to live openly in his freedom!"* Paul says, just because we're under grace and we're free from the "tyranny" of the old covenant does not mean we can do anything we want. The freedom that God offers is the freedom from sin. God offers freedom from sin through His grace.

Romans 6:14-23 KJV, *"For sin shall not have dominion over you: for ye are not under the law, but under grace. What then? shall we sin, because we are not under the law, but under grace? God forbid. Know ye not, that to whom ye yield yourselves servants to obey, his servants ye are to whom ye obey; whether of sin unto death, or of obedience unto righteousness? But God be thanked, that ye were the servants of sin, but ye have obeyed from the heart that form of doctrine which was delivered you. Being then made free from sin, ye became the servants of righteousness. I speak after the manner of men because of the infirmity of your flesh: for as ye have yielded your members servants to uncleanness and to iniquity unto iniquity; even so now yield your members servants to righteousness unto holiness. For when ye were the servants of sin, ye were free from righteousness. What fruit had ye then in those things whereof ye are now ashamed? for the end of those things is death. But now being made free from sin, and become servants to God, ye have your fruit unto holiness, and the end everlasting life. For the wages of sin is death; but the gift of God is eternal life through Jesus Christ our Lord."* Verse 22 says there should be some "fruit unto holiness" which is the evidence of our conversion, just as our old sin nature produced the fruit that we're now ashamed of. You're not ashamed of sin until you're truly and sincerely converted. Before your conversion you boasted and bragged about your sin, and in some cases craved it like a drug addict.

Matthew 14:44-46 *"Again, the kingdom of heaven is like unto treasure hid in a field; the which when a man hath found, he hideth, and for joy thereof goeth and selleth all that he hath, and buyeth that field. Again, the kingdom of heaven is like unto a merchant man, seeking goodly pearls: Who, when he had found one pearl of great price, went and sold all that he had, and bought it."* Jesus sees the gift of salvation that He purchased as a treasure and pearl of great price, that after a man has found it, he will deny himself of everything else to possesses and keep it. That's why Jesus said deny yourself, take up our cross, and follow Him. Mark 8:34 *"And when he had called the people unto him with his disciples also, he said unto them, Whosoever will come after me, let him deny himself, and take up his cross, and follow me."*

I believe what Jesus would and will say to those who continue to sin is found in Matthew 7:21-23. *"Not every one that saith unto me, Lord, Lord, shall enter into the kingdom of heaven; but he that doeth the will of my Father which is in heaven. Many will say to me in that day, Lord, Lord, have we not prophesied in thy name? and in thy name have cast out devils? and in thy name done many wonderful works? And then will I profess unto them, I never knew you: depart from me, ye that work iniquity."*

It seems like a lot of People want Jesus to be their savior but not their Lord. The word Lord means: the owner; one who has control of the person, the master, as in landlord. My mom used to tell me to make Jesus my Lord and not just my savior. The people mentioned in Matthew 7:21-23 may have made Jesus their savior, and understood the power and authority in His name. That's why they had the ability to operate in the gifts of the Spirit, cast out devils, and to do many wonderful works in His name. But in spite of all that, Jesus professed to them I NEVER KNEW YOU, and called their works iniquity.

Jesus said, Jesus said, *"Not every one that saith unto me, Lord, Lord, shall enter into the kingdom of heaven; but he that doeth the will of my Father which is in heaven."* Even Satan knows that Jesus is Lord, but he's not submitted to doing God's will. The evidence of Jesus being your Lord is your submission and obedience to His Word and Will. Some people are their own lord, and they use grace as their excuse for doing whatever they want.

JESUS IS LORD! The question is: is Jesus your Lord? One day soon, every knee shall bow and every tongue will confess that Jesus is Lord.

If Jesus were here would He say; *"sin no more, lest a worse thing come unto the"* (John 5:14). Would Jesus say; *"go, and sin no more"* (John 8:11), or would He say; *"And why call me, Lord, Lord, and do not the things which I say?"* (Luke 6:46) I believe He would say all of that and more.

Jesus is Lord, and Jesus is the Word. It seems like some people have made Paul Lord, and they're following him instead of Jesus.

67

THE WAGES OF SIN

Romans 6:23 says, *"For the wages of sin is death; but the gift of God is eternal life through Jesus Christ our Lord."* According to Romans 6:23 the wages of sin is death. This verse is written in the New Testament, to New Covenant, saved by grace believers. So the question is: are the wages of sin still death? The word death is referring to physical and spiritual death. The Strongs Concordance says **"with the implied idea of future misery in hell."**

I believe sin still produces death (physical & spiritual), just as the Word of God says. Satan loves the idea of us only being concerned with whether or not we can lose our salvation while seemingly ignoring all of the other consequences of sin. Even if grace will keep you from losing your salvation, sin will still cause you to lose everything else. Born Again, Spirit filled people have lost their families, ministries, and even their lives, because of sin. It's a trick of the enemy to get us so focused on the loss of our salvation that we become totally oblivious to the other consequences of sin.

Not long ago a few well-known "Televangelists" sinned. As a result of their indiscretions they lost their families and ministries. Their actions also cast a shadow of suspicion and mistrust on television ministries that still exist today. Some people even claimed to have lost their faith as a result of these ministry scandals. So although losing your salvation could be the greatest consequence of sin, it is far from the only consequence. In Acts 2:1-10 Ananias and his wife Sapphira dropped dead after lying to the Holy Ghost. I don't know if Ananias and Sapphira lost their salvation, but they definitely lost their lives.

Grace did not remove the wages of sin. Grace gave us the ability not to sin, and the ability too be forgiven if we do. One of the definitions of sin is: to miss the mark. My question is; why would you want to just keep missing the mark? In any other arena, that would be considered insanity. The grace of God is not so that we can keep missing the mark, over, and over, and over, and over again. The grace of God enables us to measure up and consistently hit the mark.

The belief that grace will keep you from being separated from God when you sin does not encourage more people to be saved, nor does it help people to live a sinless life as some preachers have claimed. Jude 3 & 4 calls that a distortion of grace, and turning the grace of God into lasciviousness. *"Beloved, when I gave all diligence to write unto you of the common salvation, it was needful for me to write unto you, and exhort you that ye should earnestly contend for the faith which was once delivered unto the saints. For there are certain men crept in unawares, who were before of old ordained to this condemnation, ungodly men, turning the grace of our God into lasciviousness, and denying the only Lord God, and our Lord Jesus Christ."*

Jude 1:4 (AMP) *"For certain people have crept in unnoticed [just as if they were sneaking in by a side door]. They are ungodly persons whose condemnation was predicted long ago, for they distort the grace of our God into decadence and immoral freedom [viewing it as an opportunity to do whatever they want], and deny and disown our only Master and Lord, Jesus Christ."*

Jude 1:4 (GNT) *"For some godless people have slipped in unnoticed among us, persons who distort the message about the grace of our God in order to excuse their immoral ways, and who reject Jesus Christ, our only Master and Lord. Long ago the Scriptures predicted the condemnation they have received."*

WHAT IS SIN?

The word sin in Romans 6:23 is translated from the Greek word **hamartia** which means: offence sin(ful): to be without a share in: to miss the mark: to err, be mistaken: to miss or wonder from the path of uprightness and honor, to do or go wrong: to wander from the law of God, a violation of the divine law in thought or in act, sin.

1 John 3:4 says, *"sin is the transgression of the law."* I've never heard anyone say that Adam and Eve transgressed the law. Most of the time we simply say Adam sinned, or Adam disobeyed God. So, I think a simple definition of sin is disobedience.

When Lucifer rebelled against God, and when the people of Sodom and Gomorrah committed abominations, there were no laws against what they had done, but it was considered sin, and the consequence of that sin was death (spiritual & physical).

2 Peter 2:4-6 says, *"For if God spared not the angels that sinned, but cast them down to hell, and delivered them into chains of darkness, to be reserved unto judgment; And spared not the old world, but saved Noah the eighth person, a preacher of righteousness, bringing in the flood upon the world of the ungodly; And turning the cities of Sodom and Gomorrah into ashes condemned them with an overthrow, making them an ensample unto those that after should live ungodly."* These verses tell us that the fallen angels, the people of Noah's day, and the people of Sodom and Gomorrah are examples for us as to what happens to people who are not under the Law when they sin.

James 4:17 says *"Therefore to him that knoweth to do good, and doeth it not, to him it is sin."* I believe God put it in us to know good and bad, right and wrong. That's why a young child will lie when asked if he did something wrong, even if they've never been told it's wrong. The lying is the evidence of the sin nature, but the reason they lie is because somehow they knew it was wrong. 1 John 3:19-21 (AMP) says, *"By this we will know [without any doubt] that we are of the truth, and will assure our heart and quiet our conscience before Him whenever our heart convicts us [in guilt]; for God is greater than our heart and He knows all things [nothing is hidden from Him because we are in His hands]. Beloved, if our heart does not convict us [of guilt], we have confidence [complete assurance and boldness] before God."* This is why Cain lied about knowing where Abel his brother was. There was no Law against murder, but Cane knew it was wrong. Genesis 4:9 (AMP), *Then the Lord said to Cain, "Where is Abel your brother?" And he [lied and] said, "I do not know. Am I my brother's keeper?"*

The giving of the Law didn't make it possible to sin. People were sinning before the Law. The Law came and increased our consciousness of sin. Cain and Abel are another example of people sinning who were not under the Law, and that sin causing their separation from God.

CAN YOU LOSE YOUR SALVATION?

I probably should have made this the first chapter of the book, because this is what you really want to know, and you're probably starting here anyhow.

I will start by saying that I believe the term **"you can't lose your salvation"** is the same thing as saying **your sin won't separate you from God.** I say that, because sin is what caused us to be separated from God, and salvation reconciled and brought us back into fellowship with Him. Everyone that I've ever heard use the term "you can't lose your salvation," was always using it in reference to a Born Again Christian losing his salvation (being separated from God) as a result of committing sin.

I do believe you can *'lose'* your salvation, but not for the traditional reasons that are usually given. I believe you can abandon, relinquish, forfeit, or give up your salvation any time you choose to do so. That's what happens when Born Again Christians decide to leave Christianity and convert to some other religion, and when they willfully and intentionally commit sin.

The first thing wrong with the idea of whether or not you can lose your salvation is, the use of the word lose. The word lose describes something that is done unintentionally, or something done by mistake. Losing your salvation would be like coming home from shopping and realizing that you don't have your wallet. You don't know how, when, or where you lost it, but it's gone. A better way to phrase it might be; is it possible to forfeit your salvation, or to relinquish your salvation? Relinquish means: to renounce or surrender (a possession, right, etc.): to give up; put aside or desist from: to let go; release. Another word might be abandon, or even give up. Abandon means: to leave completely; forsake utterly; to give up; discontinue; withdraw from. If

71

someone asked; can you give up, abandon, relinquish, or forsake your salvation, what would you say? Your answer might be different than what you would say if asked; can you lose your salvation? I think using one of those words puts the idea in the proper perspective, because the loss of your salvation now becomes something being done intentionally as an act of a person's freewill. That's what I mean when I refer to willful, intentional sin. It's something done as a deliberate act of your freewill. When there was no Mosaic or Levitical Law, Adam deliberately, intentionally sinned and lost everything as a result. Eve was deceived Adam was not. Adam's sin was a deliberate, intentional act of his freewill.

The question of whether or not you can lose your salvation is definitely one of thee most important issues facing the Body of Christ today. For years people have argued about prosperity, water baptism, and the gifts of the Spirit, but when it comes to our salvation, now you're talking about the very foundation of our relationship with God and our eternal habitation. Just think about what the consequences will be for millions of people if you get this wrong. I don't believe God is giving and taking salvation from people with every sin or mistake they make, but I do believe that a willful, continual, intentional practice of sin will cause you to forfeit the gift of salvation and be separated from God. That's what happened from Genesis to Revelations, and God doesn't change. (*"I change not."* Malachi 3:6)

The question of whether or not you can lose your salvation is something that we just can't afford to get wrong!

When I prayed and sought the Lord about the doctrine of eternal security, one of the things He told me was; the doctrine of not being able to lose your salvation is not new. He said; the first person to teach it was Satan in the Garden of Eden. Satan said to the woman "Ye shall not surely die." Satan was telling the woman that her sin would not bring death, natural or spiritual. That's the same thing many people are teaching today; that sin won't separate you from God, and they use grace as the reason why. Today, this doctrine has taken on several clever names. Eternal security, eternal salvation, once saved always saved, and you can't lose your salvation, to name a few. It's the same message that Satan preached in the Garden of Eden, just being presented with clever, deceptive titles.

The forfeiting of your salvation is a process. You don't bounce in and out of salvation every time you make a mistake. The process begins with a willful, deliberate act of sin, just as it did in the Garden of Eden. Genesis 6:5-6 says, *"And God saw that the wickedness of man was great in the earth, and that every imagination of the thoughts of his*

72

heart was only evil continually. And it repented the Lord that he had made man on the earth, and it grieved him at his heart." It was man's **continual** wickedness and evil that grieved God and brought about man's destruction in the flood. With Adam and Eve it was a single act of disobedience that brought about their separation from God just as He told them it would. Adam and Eve, the people of Noah's day, and the people of Sodom and Gomorrah all committed deliberate acts of rebellion or sin. I can't find anywhere in the Old or New Testament where there were no consequences for deliberate acts of sin. Ananias and Sapphira are New Testament examples of that in Acts 5. Anyone who uses grace as the reason that you can't lose your salvation, or once saved always saved; doesn't understand what grace is.

Jesus said, His sheep know His voice and follow Him. Knowing His voice comes as a result of relationship, following is done by choice. Sheep get lost when they choose to stop following the shepherd. Sometimes this happens by choice and other times, because they were led astray. Being led astray doesn't necessarily mean they were plucked out of the shepherd's hand, it just means they allowed something or someone to influence their choice in the way they would go. Adam and Eve belonged to God and they were led astray, because Eve was deceived. Adam chose to follow Eve, even though he knew what God said.

John 10:27-29 says, *"My sheep hear my voice, and I know them, and they follow me: And I give unto them eternal life; and they shall never perish, neither shall any man pluck them out of my hand. My Father, which gave them me, is greater than all; and no man is able to pluck them out of my Father's hand."* No one can take you out of God's hand, and no one can put you in God's hand, or make you stay in God's hand against your freewill.

Once you're saved, born again, forgiven of your sin, etc., no one can take that from you. No one can take you out of the hand of Jesus, and no one can take you out of the hand of God the Father. But, what happens if you decide you know longer want to walk with the Lord? What if you decide you don't want to be in God's hand anymore? I believe you can take yourself out of God's hand whenever you want. In John 6 there were disciples that turned their back on Jesus and stopped walking with Him. *"Many therefore of his disciples, when they had heard this, said, This is an hard saying; who can hear it?" "From that time many of his disciples went back, and walked no more with him. Then said Jesus unto the twelve, "Will ye also go away? Then Simon Peter answered him, Lord, to whom shall we go?*

73

thou hast the words of eternal life." (John 6:60-68) They were able to stop walking with Jesus, because they had freewill. The twelve disciples that continued to walk with Jesus did so, because He had the Words of eternal life. If you think God is allowing people in His hand to willfully practice sin, then you don't understand God's hand or His nature.

Jesus said, *"My sheep hear my voice, and I know them, and they follow me."* I think this is a very important. First of all, you hear His voice because you're His and you're listening. Secondly, He knows you, and third, you follow Him. The evidence that you're in His hand is that you're following Him. How can you be in His hand and be going in a different direction?

Romans 6:16-19 says, whomever you yield yourself to that's whose servant you are. I could say; who ever you're following, that's whose servant you are, because following is a sign of being yielded and obedience.

"Know ye not, that to whom ye yield yourselves servants to obey, his servants ye are to whom ye obey; whether of sin unto death, or of obedience unto righteousness? But God be thanked, that ye were the servants of sin, but ye have obeyed from the heart that form of doctrine which was delivered you. Being then made free from sin, ye became the servants of righteousness. I speak after the manner of men because of the infirmity of your flesh: for as ye have yielded your members servants to uncleanness and to iniquity unto iniquity; even so now yield your members servants to righteousness unto holiness." Who you follow determines the fruit you produce, whether sin or righteousness. If you're in God's hand you should be producing righteousness not death. Can you be in God's hand and not be yielded and obedient to Him? God's hand represents His strength, His will, His works, His Kingdom, His Word, etc. None of those things produce death. That's why in Matthew 7:20 Jesus said, *"Wherefore by their fruits ye shall know them."* Amos 3:3 says, *"Can two walk together, except they be agreed?"*

Matthew 7:18 says, *"A good tree cannot bring forth evil fruit, neither can a corrupt tree bring forth good fruit."* So, can a tree change the type of fruit it's producing, and if it does, is that the evidence that the tree has changed? Yes! That's what happens when someone is born again. The change in fruit is the evidence of conversion. From evil to good fruit, or from death to life.

Willful, continual sin creates a hard heart. Evidence of a hard heart is: insensitivity to the conviction of the Holy Spirit, dulling of the Spiritual senses, and a loss of desire to fellowship with God just to name a few. A

74

hardened heart is portrayed as a heart that has become callused as a result of continued disobedience, or ongoing rebellion. The friction of sin and disobedience has created a callus on the heart (inner man, inward seat of the soul), making it insensitive to the conviction of the Holy Spirit. So Jesus says harden not your heart. In other words He's saying, don't continue to disobey and sin, because it will produce a hard heart, callused and insensitive.

If you don't believe you can lose your salvation you probably will, or you possibly already have. I say that, because most of the people that I know who believe you can't lose your salvation usually confuse conviction with condemnation, and if you can't be convicted, then you'll never seek to be forgiven, and you'll never repent (change).

I heard a preacher ask; **CAN YOU UNDO WHAT JESUS DID?** Well, the answer is no: you can't undo what Jesus did when it comes to His death, burial, and resurrection, but you can, by an act of your freewill, make a decision to stop following Jesus if you want to. Jesus purchased our salvation. We chose to receive it by grace through faith. So maybe a better question would be; **can you undo what you did?** Hebrews 4 answers that question, and I discuss that in a section of the book titled The Qualifications.

As long as you have freewill you can choose to reject, renounce, or deny Jesus any time you want. People don't lose their salvation they leave it. Jesus said, no man is able to pluck us out of his hand or out of His Father's hand, but that doesn't mean you can't decide to pluck yourself out of God's hand whenever you want. Judas did it, and Simon Peter did it when his faith failed and he denied Jesus three times. That's why Jesus said to him *"But I have prayed for thee, that thy faith fail not: and when thou art converted, strengthen thy brethren."* (Luke 22:32) The word converted is translated from the Greek word epistrepho, which means: to return to: to cause to return: to turn one's self about, turn back. Some may argue about what happened when Peter's faith failed, but if it didn't fail and he wasn't lost just as Judas was, then there would be no need for conversion, just restoration.

I'm amazed at how upset and angry people get when I suggest that they can lose their salvation. It makes me wonder why they're so upset, because the idea of losing my salvation doesn't bother me at all. Maybe it's because I'm trusting God to give me grace to keep me from falling, as opposed to believing God will give me grace and allow me to keep sinning and remain saved.

I CHANGE NOT

Malachi 3:6 says, *"For I am the Lord, I change not,"* and Hebrews 13:8 says, *"Jesus Christ the same yesterday, and to day, and for ever."* God doesn't change, and He hasn't changed. He is **THE SAME** yesterday, and today, and forever. So, in order for us to sin and that sin not separate us from God, He would have to change. God has always been a God of grace, but He has never allowed sin in His Kingdom or presence, and He never will!

In order for the doctrines of "you can't lose your salvation," "eternal security," or once saved always saved" to be true, God would have to change His nature and character, not just His covenant. I think we've overlooked the fact that when we are born again we become citizens of the Kingdom of Heaven, and God has never allowed sin in His Kingdom. Jesus, in the New Testament introduced a change in covenant not a change in God's character. If Eve had considered God's character, she would have realized that God wouldn't lie or change His Word. The immutable nature and character of God is one of the major keys that have been left out of the eternal security debate. It would take more than a change of covenant for God to allow sin to be practiced in His Kingdom. I am the LORD, I change not, is God establishing forever that He does not change. This alone is enough to prove that you cannot willfully, intentionally commit sin and remain in the Kingdom of God. Hebrews 5:9 says, *"And being made perfect, he became the author of eternal salvation <u>unto all them that obey him.</u>"* Jesus is the author of eternal salvation to all that obey Him. Obedience is something that God has always required in His Kingdom, and that hasn't changed. The grace of God enables us to be saved, repent, and obey God.

Ananias and his wife Sapphira dropped dead after lying to the Holy Ghost, because although God changed His covenant He did not change His Nature.

SEALED

Some people claim that it's impossible for a person to lose their salvation, because they've been sealed.

The word sealed is translated from the Greek word sphragizo, and is used seventeen times in the New Testament. It means: 1) to set a seal upon, mark with a seal, to seal

76

a) for security: from satan
b) since things sealed up are concealed (as the contents of a letter), to hide, keep in silence, keep secret
c) In order to mark a person or a thing
1) to set a mark upon by the impress of a seal or stamp
2) angels are said to be sealed by God
   b) in order to prove, confirm, or attest a thing
1) to confirm, authenticate, place beyond doubt
   a) of a written document
b) to prove one's testimony to a person that he is what he professes to be.

As I consider the definition of the word sealed and the context in which it's being used in the scriptures, I don't feel that God is trying to tell us that being sealed makes it impossible for us to lose our salvation. I think the word sealed is describing a mark of authentication and confirmation of our salvation, and represents our security and protection from Satan. In Revelations 7:2-3, that's what being sealed represented. It was a mark of authentication and protection from the destruction that will be happening on the earth at that time.

"And I saw another angel ascending from the east, having the seal of the living God: and he cried with a loud voice to the four angels, to whom it was given to hurt the earth and the sea, Saying, Hurt not the earth, neither the sea, nor the trees, till we have sealed the servants of our God in their foreheads."

In Matthew 7:20 Jesus said, *"Wherefore by their fruits ye shall know them."* And 1John 3:7 says, *"Little children, let no man deceive you: he that doeth righteousness is righteous, even as he is righteous."*
If you want to know if you're saved or not, these two verses are a good way to determine your spiritual status. Check your fruit and whether or not you're doing righteousness. Some people would call that legalism, but it is what the Bible says in the New Testament, and as of right now, I'm not aware of a test for detecting a seal.

THE QUALIFICATIONS

Hebrews 6:4-8 tells us the process that leads to losing your salvation and needing to be forgiven, repent, and be restored back in to fellowship with God. The process has five steps and they're all mentioned in these verses. I know that there are people who have reasons for not taking these verses at face value, but I take the position of looking for confirmation of the scripture, not explaining it away. It appears that a person can come to a place where they have lost fellowship with God and need to repent, and be forgiven.

1 If they were enlightened (Jesus has been revealed to them by the Holy Spirit).

2 if they have tasted of the heavenly gift (they've received salvation, been converted).

3 They've received the gift of the Holy Ghost.

4 They've received supernatural revelation knowledge of God's Word.

5 They have seen and operated in the gifts of the Spirit.

1 John 1:9-10 is speaking to believers that sin, not unbelievers. We, born again believers, have to confess our sins, and then God cleanses us. *"If we confess our sins, he is faithful and just to forgive us our sins, and to cleanse us from all unrighteousness. If we say that we have not sinned, we make him a liar, and his word is not in us."*

Hebrews 6 speaks about the idea of being Born Again after you were Born Again.

Hebrews 6:4-8 (MSG), *"Once people have seen the light, gotten a taste of heaven and been part of the work of the Holy Spirit, once they've personally experienced the sheer goodness of God's Word and the powers breaking in on us—if then they turn their backs on it, washing their hands of the whole thing, well, they can't start over as if nothing happened. That's impossible. Why, they've re-crucified Jesus! They've repudiated him in public! Parched ground that soaks up the rain and then produces an abundance of carrots and corn for its gardener gets God's "Well done!" But if it produces weeds and thistles, it's more likely to get cussed out. Fields like that are burned, not harvested."*

1. If they turn there back on it (you can turn your back on your salvation).
2. They can't start over as if nothings happened (you can't start over or keep going as if nothings happened).
3. The tree is known by the fruit it produces.

Hebrews 6:4-8 (AMP) *"For [it is impossible to restore to repentance] those who have once been enlightened [spiritually] and who have tasted and consciously experienced the heavenly gift and have shared in the Holy Spirit, and have tasted and consciously experienced the good word of God and the powers of the age (world) to come, and then have fallen away--it is impossible to bring them back again to repentance, since they again nail the Son of God on the cross [for as far as they are concerned, they are*

78

treating the death of Christ as if they were not saved by it], and are holding Him up again to public disgrace. For soil that drinks the rain which often falls on it and produces crops useful to those for whose benefit it is cultivated, receives a blessing from God; but if it persistently produces thorns and thistles, it is worthless and close to being cursed, and it ends up being burned." This verse says, *"if it persistently produces thorns and thistles, it is worthless."* This is saying that you can't get born again and continue to persistently practice sin. Jesus said *"Ye shall know them by their fruits,"* and sin produces thorns and thistles (Matthew 7:16).

This is not just a description of someone who's been born again. This also describes the state that Adam and Eve were in before they sinned. Their spirits were as our spirits become when we're born again. So if their sin brought death, so does ours! *"Once people have seen the light, 2) gotten a taste of heaven 3) and been part of the work of the Holy Spirit, 4) once they've personally experienced the sheer goodness of God's Word and the powers breaking in on us."* Adam and Eve couldn't just keep going or start over as if nothing happened.

Some people don't believe that these passages of scripture mean that people can turn their back on their salvation or fall away from their relationship with the Holy Spirit, even though it appears to clearly state that. They believe these passages are saying the exact opposite. They say that these scriptures are saying it's impossible for a person to fall away once they've seen the light and experience the Holy Spirit. My answer to that is; **Adam and Eve did it, and born again, Spirit filled Christians do it all the time.** It's possible, because it's been done and being done all the time.

My dilemma is, I read the Bible and believe it says what it means and means what it says. I believe revelation comes to confirm and establish the Word, not to explain it away and say it doesn't mean that. All of the translations that I've studied confirm and establish my point of view. So, after careful consideration I've decided to take what the Bible is saying at face value and believe it means exactly what it says. Satan came to Eve and gave her a false, deceptive revelation of what God said. I pay attention if someone says, "I know the Bible says this, but this is what it really means." That's not revelation, that's deception. That's a **"hath God said"** for sure!

THE UNFORGIVEN SERVANT

Not long ago the Lord gave me a revelation about the parable in Matthew 18:23-35. In this parable the king comes and begins to take account of his servants. As the king is reckoning a servant was brought to him which owed him ten thousand talents, and because the servant didn't have the ability to repay the debt, it was commanded that he, his wife, his children and all that he had should be sold, and that payment should be made from the proceeds of the sale

Matthew 18:23-35 says, *"Therefore is the kingdom of heaven likened unto a certain king, which would take account of his servants. And when he had begun to reckon, one was brought unto him, which owed him ten thousand talents. But forasmuch as he had not to pay, his lord commanded him to be sold, and his wife, and children, and all that he had, and payment to be made. The servant therefore fell down, and worshipped him, saying, Lord, have patience with me, and I will pay thee all. Then the lord of that servant was moved with compassion, and loosed him, and forgave him the debt. But the same servant went out, and found one of his fellowservants, which owed him an hundred pence: and he laid hands on him, and took him by the throat, saying, Pay me that thou owest.*

And his fellowservant fell down at his feet, and besought him, saying, Have patience with me, and I will pay thee all. And he would not: but went and cast him into prison, till he should pay the debt. So when his fellowservants saw what was done, they were very sorry, and came and told unto their lord all that was done. Then his lord, after that he had called him, said unto him, O thou wicked servant, I forgave thee all that debt, because thou desiredst me: Shouldest not thou also have had compassion on thy fellowservant, even as I had pity on thee? And his lord was wroth, and delivered him to the tormentors, till he should pay all that was due unto him. So likewise shall my heavenly Father do also unto you, if ye from your hearts forgive not every one his brother their trespasses."

In this parable the servant was forgiven of all the debt that he was unable to pay as an act of grace. He didn't deserve to be forgiven, he couldn't earn it, and would never have worthy to receive forgiveness, but the king forgave him as an act of grace. It was a gift. Later on in the parable, this same servant found a fellow servant which owed him money that he was unable to pay, but instead of freely forgiving his fellow servant, he put his hands around his throat and choked him, and then had him put into prison until he had repaid all that he owed. As a result of this wicked act, the king was angry and took back his gift and act of grace. The King had the servant and his family sent to the tormenters to pay the debt that he had previously been forgiven of.

I believe God is showing us through this parable that you can be forgiven by an act of God's grace, and then lose that gift through sin, which in this case was his unwillingness to forgive. **Can a gift and act of grace be overturned or undone?** In this case it was.

CAN YOU UNDO WHAT JESUS DID?

I've heard people say, "you didn't save yourself, Jesus purchased your salvation, and you can't undo what Jesus did for you." I totally agree with that; you cannot undo what Jesus did for you at Calvary. You can't undo the scourging, the nailing to the cross, the blood that He shed, or His death, burial and resurrection. All of that is what Jesus did for us to purchase our salvation, and it can't ever be undone; HALLELUJAH!

I do believe however that we can undo what we did anytime we want by an act of our freewill. Being saved doesn't override your freewill. You're saved by grace through faith. Salvation is a gift from God in response to your faith and confession. But if you decide to no longer follow Him, you can renounce and reject Him whenever you want, because you still have freewill.

In the parable of Matthew 18:23, the servant lost or undid the gift of forgiveness and debt cancellation that he received when he sinned and refused to forgive his fellow servant. It is clear in this parable that the King took back the gift of grace and forgiveness that was given to his servant. The servant was then left with the responsibility of paying all of his own sin debt.

Isaiah 43:25 says, **"I, even I, am he that blotteth out thy transgressions for mine own sake, and will not remember thy sins."** Based on this verse you might be thinking that, unlike the servant in this parable we can't be held responsible to pay something that God has blotted out and forgotten; and you're right! If we sin, we do not become responsible to pay for passed, confessed, forgiven sin, but we are responsible for the sins we commit after we're forgiven. Being forgiven doesn't mean I'm not responsible for future sin. That's why if you sin, you have to confess and be forgiven. 1 John 1:9 says, **"If we confess our sins, he is faithful and just to forgive us our sins, and to cleanse us from all unrighteousness."** 1 John 1:9, is written to born again believers, people walking in the light with God. The Amplified Version says, **"He is faithful and just [true to His own nature and** *promises]."* God will always be true to His nature. He will forgive if we confess, but He will not allow sin in His Kingdom. That would go against His nature.

Sin separates us from God. Salvation brings the sinner back into fellowship with God by grace through faith in Jesus Christ. Does sin separate a person from God after they've received the gift of salvation? Well, if you believe that God covers your sin with grace then no, but if you believe that grace is not the covering of your sin, but rather the ability to freely receive forgiveness of your sin, and the empowerment to overcome sin, then yes. Obviously I believe the later.

The word **debt** used in Matthew 18:27, is translated from the Greek word daneion. This word refers to a debt that cannot be repaid, and is only used here in Matthew 18:27. The word debt that is used in Matthew 18:30 and other places in the scripture is translated from the Greek word opheilo, which means to owe, or to be in debt. This word is referring to a debt that a person could possibly pay off. So, the story is speaking of two types of debt: one that is possible for a person to pay, and one that a person could never pay. This parable is a picture of someone forfeiting his salvation.

When we're born again, we are restored back to where Adam and Eve were spiritually before sin. We are born again; they were created that way. We need to be born again of incorruptible seed, because sin corrupted everyone born after Adam sinned. So if sin could corrupt Adam and Eve's spirit it can corrupt or born again spirit as well, because our spirits are the same as theirs were in the Garden of Eden.

Satan and one third of the angels sinned and rebelled against God. When they did, they were immediately cast out of Heaven. Satan and the angels weren't under the Law, neither were Adam and Eve, but when they sinned they could no longer be in God's presence. God's answer to their sin was not grace to keep sinning, and that's not His answer now. God gave us grace to be forgiven, and grace to overcome sin.

One of the things that you have to consider is; what is salvation? Dictionary.com defines **salvation** as; **deliverance from the power and penalty of sin; redemption: deliverance by redemption from the power of sin and from the penalties ensuing from it.** So, people who believe you can't lose your salvation are basically saying; salvation brought you deliverance from the penalty of sin, but not the

82

power of sin. They believe grace allows you to keep doing the thing that salvation should have delivered you from. I believe salvation by grace through faith delivers you from the power and penalties of sin, not just the penalties.

John 15:5-6 Jesus said, *"I am the vine, ye are the branches: He that abideth in me, and I in him, the same bringeth forth much fruit: for without me ye can do nothing. If a man abide not in me, he is cast forth as a branch, and is withered; and men gather them, and cast them into the fire, and they are burned."* Jesus is the Word, and the Word is Jesus. So when we're walking with Jesus we're walking with and in the Word. Abiding in the Word means you're doing what it says. If you refuse to forgive, then you're not abiding in the Word.

1 John 3:1-10 says, *"Behold, what manner of love the Father hath bestowed upon us, that we should be called the sons of God: therefore the world knoweth us not, because it knew him not. Beloved, now are we the sons of God, and it doth not yet appear what we shall be: but we know that, when he shall appear, we shall be like him; for we shall see him as he is. And every man that hath this hope in him purifieth himself, even as he is pure. Whosoever committeth sin transgresseth also the law: for sin is the transgression of the law. And ye know that he was manifested to take away our sins; and in him is no sin. Whosoever abideth in him sinneth not: whosoever sinneth hath not seen him, neither known him. Little children, let no man deceive you: he that doeth righteousness is righteous, even as he is righteous. He that committeth sin is of the devil; for the devil sinneth from the beginning. For this purpose the Son of God was manifested, that he might destroy the works of the devil. Whosoever is born of God doth not commit sin; for his seed remaineth in him: and he cannot sin, because he is born of God. In this the children of God are manifest, and the children of the devil: whosoever doeth not righteousness is not of God, neither he that loveth not his brother."*

"Whosoever abideth in him sinneth not." This is not because we're no longer under the Law. This is because Him, Jesus, is the Word made flesh, and as long as you're doing the Word you can't sin. If you refuse to *"Love your enemies, bless them that curse you, do good to them that hate you, and pray for them which despitefully use you, and persecute you"* (Matthew 5:44), then you're not abiding in the Word. If you're not in the Word then you're in the flesh, and the flesh reaps corruption. Galatians 6:8 *"For he that soweth to his flesh shall of the flesh reap corruption; but he that soweth to the Spirit shall of the*

Spirit reap life everlasting." Corruption is translated from the Greek word phthora which means: in the Christian sense, eternal misery in hell: in an ethical sense, corruption i.e. moral decay. Also, *"for his seed remaineth in him"* is not the Holy Spirit. The seed is the Word. The Holy Spirit will not dwell in a defiled temple, He will destroy it according to 1 Corinthians 3:16-17. *"Know ye not that ye are the temple of God, and that the Spirit of God dwelleth in you? If any man defile the temple of God, him shall God destroy; for the temple of God is holy, which temple ye are."*

The words defile and destroy are translated from the Greek word phtheiro which means: to corrupt, to destroy, to perish: to lead away a Christian church from that state of knowledge and holiness in which it ought to abide.

THE FIRST THING

Many years ago, a co-worker came to me and asked if it were possible to lose your salvation. At that time, although I believed the answer was yes, I went home and asked my dad, who was also my pastor, and he agreed. Since then, I've heard teachings and read books that seem to be pretty divided on the subject. After I became a pastor, I found myself responsible for answering this question for the souls that had been entrusted to me. So, I did the only thing any good pastor would do, I prayed and asked the Lord. As a matter of fact, I asked Him several times. The reason I asked Him several times is, because I wanted confirmation; I needed to be sure. I believe God always confirms His Word, and the Bible says; in the presence of two or three witnesses everything is established. I didn't search the scriptures to prove my point of view. I simply asked God and allowed Him to answer me, and then confirm and establish His answers with His Word. The exciting thing is, each time I asked Him He gave me an answer, and confirmed and established it with His Word just as I had hoped He would. This book is the result of that.

The first thing He told me was that the message of not being able to lose your salvation was not a new message or doctrine, but that it was an old message, and Satan was the first one to preach it in the Garden of Eden. The woman, Eve, was the first person to be told that her sin wouldn't result in death; physical, spiritual, and the second death. In Eve's case the consequence of her sin was immediate spiritual death, which is separation from God. Adam and Eve also lost their authority, their home in the Garden of Eden, and their immortality.

84

Genesis 3:1-5 *Now the serpent was more subtil than any beast of the field which the Lord God had made. And he said unto the woman, Yea, hath God said, Ye shall not eat of every tree of the garden? And the woman said unto the serpent, We may eat of the fruit of the trees of the garden: But of the fruit of the tree which is in the midst of the garden, God hath said, Ye shall not eat of it, neither shall ye touch it, lest ye die. And the serpent said unto the woman, Ye shall not surely die: For God doth know that in the day ye eat thereof, then your eyes shall be opened, and ye shall be as gods, knowing good and evil.* Satan told Eve the same thing that's being taught by many preachers today. They may not be using the exact same words, but the message is the same, and the results will be the same as well.

THE SECOND THING

The second thing God told me was that Jesus and Paul's teachings on sin were not different. I've heard it said that Jesus and Paul taught differently about sin, because they were talking to two different audiences. Some say that Jesus was talking to Old Testament Jews still under the law, and Paul was talking to New Testament believers who were under grace. There are several reasons that I can't agree with that idea, but the main reason is, because God said it wasn't true.

1. Grace and truth came by Jesus, so everything He taught and did was by grace, through grace, and about grace; for the purpose of introducing people to grace. That's why Jesus healed on the Sabbath day, didn't condemn the woman caught in adultery, and told the impotent man to carry his bed on the Sabbath. All of these things were against the law, and that's why the Scribes, Pharisees and High Priest were always condemning Him for it.
2. The disciples of Jesus didn't fast often, or wash their hands before they ate. Jesus used these things as opportunities to introduce grace.
3. Paul never said that sin no longer had consequences because of grace, or that sin would no longer separate you from God. As a matter of fact, Paul wrote that the wages of sin is death (physical, spiritual, and the second death). Paul also said that there is therefore now, no condemnation to those who are in Christ Jesus, who walk not after the flesh, but after the Spirit. One of the conditions for not being under condemnation is, not walking after the flesh, but after the spirit. Walking after the flesh is what puts you under condemnation. So if you're

still walking after the flesh, then you're still under condemnation.

Romans 8:1 KJV says, *"There is therefore now no condemnation to them which are in Christ Jesus, who walk not after the flesh, but after the Spirit."* You're either walking with Jesus or walking after the flesh. There are two conditions for not being in condemnation; being in Christ Jesus, and not walking after the flesh, but after the Spirit. So, the first step to being free from condemnation is, to be in Christ Jesus. The second step is, to stop walking after the flesh and start walking after the Spirit. I would call that conversion and repentance.

Jesus said, we must be converted in Matthew 18:3 *"And said, Verily I say unto you, Except ye be converted, and become as little children, ye shall not enter into the kingdom of heaven."*

Acts 3:19 says *"Repent ye therefore, and be converted, that your sins may be blotted out, when the times of refreshing shall come from the presence of the Lord."*

The Amplified Version says, *"So repent (change your mind and purpose); turn around and return [to God], that your sins may be erased (blotted out, wiped clean), that times of refreshing (of recovering from the effects of heat, of reviving with fresh air) may come from the presence of the Lord."*

BLOT YOUR NAME OUT OF THE BOOK

Revelation 3:3-6 says, **"Remember therefore how thou hast received and heard, and hold fast, and repent. If therefore thou shalt not watch, I will come on thee as a thief, and thou shalt not know what hour I will come upon thee. Thou hast a few names even in Sardis which have not defiled their garments; and they shall walk with me in white: for they are worthy. He that overcometh, the same shall be clothed in white raiment; and I will not blot out his name out of the book of life, but I will confess his name before my Father, and before his angels. He that hath an ear, let him hear what the Spirit saith unto the churches."**

In the New Testament, under the New Covenant, God speaks to the church at Sardis and tells them to repent. If they will not repent, He says He will come upon them as a thief. Jesus says to those who overcome, that He will not blot their name out of the book of life. Revelations 3:4 in the Amplified version says, *"But you [still] have a few people in Sardis who have not soiled their clothes [that is, contaminated their character and personal integrity with sin]; and they will walk with Me [dressed] in white, because they are worthy (righteous)."*

In the book of Exodus we find out whose names will be blotted out of the book. Exodus 32:30-33 *"And it came to pass on the morrow, that Moses said unto the people, Ye have sinned a great sin: and now I will go up unto the Lord; peradventure I shall make an atonement for your sin. And Moses returned unto the Lord, and said, Oh, this people have sinned a great sin, and have made them gods of gold. Yet now, if thou wilt forgive their sin—; and if not, blot me, I pray thee, out of thy book which thou hast written. And the Lord said unto Moses, <u>Whosoever hath sinned against me, him will I blot out of my book.</u>"*

Moses tells God to blot his name out of His book if He's not going to forgive the people of their idolatry. God then tells Moses whose names will be blotted out of His book. *"Whosoever hath sinned against me, him will I blot out of my book."* In the Old and New Testaments sin and not repenting was the bases for having your name blotted out of the Book of Life. The fact that your name can be blotted out of the Book of Life says to me that you can forfeit, undo, or relinquish your salvation. In the book of Exodus and in the book of Revelations, both of these groups of people had committed willful, continual, presumptuous sin. They knew God, knew God was real, but still blatantly, intentionally, willfully sinned. In Revelations, the people who didn't repent would have their name blotted out, and in Exodus, it is the person who knows God and has seen and experienced Him, but yet sins against Him whose name will be blotted. That's what Hebrews 4:6-8 is talking about. He said "I am the LORD, I change not.

I read a commentary that said the book was some kind of census or citizenship book, but that doesn't make any sense, because sin is the reason for blotting out a name, and God is the one doing the blotting, not the city counsel or the government. I think it's a big mistake to overlook or explain away the blotting out of names from the book of life.

CAN YOU SIN AFTER YOU'VE BEEN BORN AGAIN?

A young man came to me after church with his Bible and said, his brother in-law told him you can't lose your salvation after you're born again, because 1 John 3:9-10 says your born of God and you can't sin, because God's seed remains in you.
"Whosoever is born of God doth not commit sin; for his seed remaineth in him: and he cannot sin, because he is born of God."

Well, the scripture says *"doth not commit sin"* before it says *"can't sin."* Doth not and can't are two completely different things. Can't sin suggest that it's become impossible to sin, and that's not the case. As long as you have free will you can chose to commit sin. I've been born again for many years and occasionally I slip and sin. This verse is actually saying that you don't sin, because you can't sin. The reason you don't sin is, because God's seed remains in you.

Some people believe the seed that this verse is referring to is the Holy Spirit, but that's a mistake. God's seed in the Bible is always symbolic of His Word. In Jesus' parable of the sower, the sower sowed the word, and the seed that was in Mary's womb was the Word, Jesus. If God's Word (seed) remains in you (which means you're following it and doing it), then you don't sin and can't sin, because everything you're doing is in agreement with God's Word.
Mark 4:14 *"The sower soweth the word."*

1 John 3:10 says, *"In this the children of God are manifest, and the children of the devil: whosoever doeth not righteousness is not of God, neither he that loveth not his brother."* Verse ten tells us how to

identify the child of God from the child of the devil. It's the same way Jesus mentioned in Matthew 7:15-16, by their fruit.

Verse ten says, *"In this the children of God are manifest, and the children of the devil: whosoever doeth not righteousness is not of God, neither he that loveth not his brother."* Anyone who is not doing righteousness and loving his brother is not of God, and his unrighteousness is the evidence that God's seed is not in him. When God's Seed is in you it will produce righteousness and love for your brother. I believe God's Seed is His Word. (Jesus is the Word & the Word is Jesus). The Word of God is also the Seed that produces salvation.

We all make mistakes! As a matter of fact, Romans 3:23 says, *"For all have sinned, and come short of the glory of God."*
God did not tolerate sin or iniquity in Heaven, or in the Garden of Eden. So why would we believe that He would allow us to willfully, continually practice sin in His Kingdom now.
That's why God gave us grace; so that we could be forgiven of our sins, and also be delivered from the power of sin. God isn't giving us grace so that we can continue to use our bodies, which are His temple as instruments of unrighteousness. No, not at all! That would be completely contrary to God's nature. God gives us grace to overcome sin and live righteous lives. That's what 1 John 3:10 means. Whoever does not do righteousness is not a child of God, and the only way that you can do righteousness and live a righteous life is through grace.
Salvation brings us back into fellowship and relationship with God. Through the finished work of Jesus, we've been redeemed and restored to the place that Adam and Eve lost after they fell. We've been made to sit with Christ in Heavenly places, but that doesn't mean we can't sin. Just as Lucifer, Adam and Eve, Cain, and the people of Sodom sinned, so can we, with the same consequence.

Ecclesiastes 7:20 says, *"For there is not a just man upon earth, that doeth good, and sinneth not."*

1 John 3:6 *"Whosoever abideth in him sinneth not: whosoever sinneth hath not seen him, neither known him."* Abiding in Him is abiding in the Word. Whoever sins is not doing the Word, and has not seen or known the Word.

1 John 5:18 *"We know that whosoever is born of God sinneth not; but he that is begotten of God keepeth himself, and that wicked one toucheth him not."* If you're really born of God you keep yourself from sin; and you're able to do it, because of grace.

1 John 1:5-7 says, *"This then is the message which we have heard of him, and declare unto you, that God is light, and in him is no darkness at all. If we say that we have fellowship with him, and walk in darkness, we lie, and do not the truth: But if we walk in the light, as he is in the light, we have fellowship one with another, and the blood of Jesus Christ his Son cleanseth us from all sin."* The message is that God is light, and in Him is no darkness at all. The word darkness is translated from the Greek word scotia. It refers to the darkness due to want of light and of ignorance of divine things. It's also associated with wickedness and the resultant misery in hell. The chapter goes on to say that if we say that we have fellowship with him, and walk in darkness, we lie, and do not the truth. So, if you say that you have fellowship with God, but you're walking in darkness or ignorance of divine things, and it's resulting in wickedness, then the scripture says you lie, and you're not doing the truth. Notice also that the scripture says that you *"do not the truth."* It doesn't say that you don't know the truth; it says that you don't do the truth. Another translation says; *"you're not practicing the truth."* Darkness means you're not enlightened or you have no revelation. Many people know what the Word says, but they have no revelation.

1 John 1:6 (AMP) says, *"If we say that we have fellowship with Him and yet walk in the darkness [of sin], we lie and do not practice the truth.* Sin is darkness, and darkness and light cannot dwell together. Does the grace of God make it possible for light and darkness to fellowship together? No! The scripture says; in Him is no darkness at all.

1 John 3:4-10 (MSG) *"All who indulge in a sinful life are dangerously lawless, for sin is a major disruption of God's order. Surely you know that Christ showed up in order to get rid of sin. There is no sin in him, and sin is not part of his program. No one who lives deeply in Christ makes a practice of sin. None of those who do practice sin have taken a good look at Christ. They've got him all backward. So, my dear children, don't let anyone divert you from the truth. It's the person who acts right who is right, just as we see it lived out in our righteous Messiah. Those who make a practice of sin are straight from the Devil, the pioneer in the practice of sin. The Son of God entered the scene to abolish the Devil's ways. People conceived and brought into life by God don't make a practice of sin. How could they? God's seed is deep within them, making them who they are. It's not in the nature of the God-begotten to practice and parade sin. Here's how you tell the difference between God's children and the Devil's children: The one who won't practice righteous ways*

isn't from God, nor is the one who won't love brother or sister. A simple test."

The Message translation uses words like indulge, program, and practice. It's basically saying that anyone who continues to indulge, practice or make sin a part of his regular program is not righteous.

COULD JESUS HAVE SINNED?

1 Peter 1:23 says, *"Being born again, not of corruptible seed, but of incorruptible, by the word of God, which liveth and abideth for ever."*

When we receive Jesus as our savior and Lord, we are born again of incorruptible seed. The question is; could Jesus, a man born of incorruptible seed, sin and be separated from God? I believe the answer is yes! The man Jesus was tempted and could have sinned.

The Lord Jesus Christ is the Son of God. He was born of the Virgin Mary by incorruptible seed when the Holy Spirit came upon her. Luke 1:35 says, *"And the angel answered and said unto her, The Holy Ghost shall come upon thee, and the power of the Highest shall overshadow thee: therefore also that holy thing which shall be born of thee shall be called the Son of God."*

Adam is called the first man; Jesus is called the second man. 1 Corinthians 15:47 says; *"the second man is the Lord from heaven."*

Adam sinned, and his sin separated him from God. Jesus never sinned, even though He was in all points tempted. *"For we have not an high priest which cannot be touched with the feeling of our infirmities; but was in all points tempted like as we are, yet without sin."* If it were impossible for Jesus to sin, then He wasn't actually tempted. The temptation was a complete waste of time. I think the fact that the Bible says Jesus was tempted is the proof that He could have sinned.

If Jesus did sin, would His sin have separated Him from the Father? Yes! Just like Adam, His sin would have separated Him from God. Matthew 27:46 *"And about the ninth hour Jesus cried with a loud voice, saying, Eli, Eli, lama sabachthani? that is to say, My God, my God, why hast thou forsaken me?"* When Jesus was made sin for us God forsook Him. God will always separate Himself from sin. Jesus, the second man, succeeded where Adam failed!

91

Jesus never sinned, but He was made sin for us, and bore our sins in His own body on the tree. 2 Corinthians 5:21 says *"For he hath made him to be sin for us, who knew no sin; that we might be made the righteousness of God in him."*

1 Peter 2:24 says, *"Who his own self bare our sins in his own body on the tree, that we, being dead to sins, should live unto righteousness: by whose stripes ye were healed."*

When Adam sinned he was separated from God. When Jesus became sin He was forsaken of God. When a born again believer willfully, continually sins, his sin separates him from God as well. Jesus and Adam are the evidence that a man born of incorruptible seed can sin, and that sin cause him to be separated from God.

If Jesus and Adam's sin mattered, so does ours! Jesus was tempted, yet without sin. Adam sinned, but the Bible doesn't say that he was tempted. Adam's sin was an intentional act of his freewill. Adam and Jesus are a picture of our spiritual condition today. We are born again of incorruptible seed and restored to the spiritual position that Adam lost. Our sin produces the same results as Adam's sin, and the same reaction from God as when Jesus became sin for us. God change the covenant not His nature. He still does not allow sin in His Kingdom, and we are in His Kingdom.

GRACE IS NOT CHEAP

The grace of God is free, but it's not cheap; it cost Jesus His life. When we try to use the grace of God as a way to continue to commit sin after we've asked God to forgive us, we cheapen the grace of God, and we devalue and insult the suffering and sacrifice of Jesus.

It is an insult to the Lord Jesus Christ when we try to turn His grace into the ability for us to continue to do the thing that caused Him to be scourged and crucified. How dare we be so selfish to even consider our ability to continue sin and satisfy our flesh. Instead, we should be so grateful for His suffering and sacrifice that we're more than willing to deny ourselves, take up our cross and follow Him. I believe that's what Hebrews 10:29 AMP is referring to. It's like we're not esteeming the Blood and sacrifice of Jesus as highly as we ought to. If we were, the idea of denying yourself wouldn't bother us at all, and the thought of losing your salvation would be justifiable.

If we continue to sin after we receive salvation we're misusing and devaluing grace. We're trying to turn grace into a cheap mechanism through which we can fulfill the lust of our flesh, and in doing so we debase, demean, and devalue the pain, suffering, and sacrifice of The Lord Jesus Christ. The price that Jesus paid for our sin was to great for us to continue to do the very thing that caused Him to have to endure that painful sacrifice in the first place.

That's what Hebrews 10:26-29 is all about. Look at verse twenty-nine. *"For if we sin wilfully after that we have received the knowledge of the truth, there remaineth no more sacrifice for sins, But a certain fearful looking for of judgment and fiery indignation, which shall devour the adversaries. He that despised Moses' law died without mercy under two or three witnesses: 29) Of how much sorer punishment, suppose ye, shall he be thought worthy, who hath trodden under foot the Son of God, and hath counted the blood of the covenant, wherewith he was sanctified, an unholy thing, and hath done despite unto the Spirit of grace?"*

According to verse 29, the punishment for the New Testament, New Covenant, Born Again believer is worse than that of the Old Testament person who broke the Mosaic Law. The Amplified version calls it an insult to the Spirit of grace. Continuing to sin after you receive salvation is an insult to the suffering of Jesus and the grace of God. It's also evidence of not understanding the purpose and power of grace.

Matthew 10:38 (AMP) Jesus said, *"And he who does not take his cross [expressing a willingness to endure whatever may come] and follow Me [believing in Me, conforming to My example in living and, if need be, suffering or perhaps dying because of faith in Me] is not worthy of Me."*

Some people would call taking up your cross legalism and works. Jesus sees it as evidence of a worthiness of Him and His sacrifice.

THE LAW WRITTEN IN THEIR HEART & MIND

We are under a better covenant, with better promises. With this covenant, God didn't put His laws on tablets; He put them in our minds and wrote them in our hearts. I believe this is how Adam was before he sinned. God told Adam not to eat of the tree of the knowledge of good and evil, but God didn't write the commandment in stone. God simply told Adam, and in doing so, that commandment was in Adam's mind and in his heart. So, God didn't do away with the law, He just transferred it from tablets of stone to our minds and hearts. The place and purpose of the Law changed. That's why 1 John 3:20 says, *"For if our hearts condemn us, God is greater than our heart, and knoweth all things,"* because that's where God has written His law and where the Holy Spirit lives.

Hebrews 8:6-10, *"But now hath he obtained a more excellent ministry, by how much also he is the mediator of a better covenant, which was established upon better promises. For if that first covenant had been faultless, then should no place have been sought for the second. For finding fault with them, he saith, Behold, the days come, saith the Lord, when I will make a new covenant with the house of Israel and with the house of Judah: Not according to the covenant that I made with their fathers in the day when I took them by the hand to lead them out of the land of Egypt; because they continued not in my covenant, and I regarded them not, saith the Lord. For this is the covenant that I will make with the house of Israel after those days, saith the Lord; I will put my laws into their mind, and write them in their hearts: and I will be to them a God, and they shall be to me a people."*

Hebrews 10:16-18 says, *"This is the covenant that I will make with them after those days, saith the Lord, I will put my laws into their hearts, and in their minds will I write them; And their sins and iniquities will I remember no more. Now where remission of these is, there is no more offering for sin."* Hebrews 10:17 is not talking about future sins, its talking about past, confessed, forgiven sins. That's why Hebrews 10:26 says, *"For if we sin wilfully after that we have received the knowledge of the truth, there remaineth no more sacrifice for sins."* This is referring to the sins that we commit after we've been saved and empowered by grace to overcome sin.

Romans 2:14-16 says, *"For when the Gentiles, which have not the law, do by nature the things contained in the law, these, having not the law, are a law unto themselves: Which shew the work of the law written in their hearts, their conscience also bearing witness, and their thoughts the mean while accusing or else excusing one another;) In the day when God shall judge the secrets of men by Jesus Christ according to my gospel."* Before the Law was written on tablets it was written in men's hearts and minds. This is called our conscience or our heart. So like Adam, Eve, and people born before the Law was given, we are back to knowing what's morally right and wrong by the Holy Spirit convicting us through our conscience, or our heart. Verse 14 says that Gentiles do by nature or by their conscience the things that are written in the Law. So, under grace, we are like the Gentiles without the law, doing by nature the things contained in the law. Not to achieve righteousness, but rather to live moral lives that are pleasing to God.

If grace is reigning as it says in Romans, then any sin that you commit after that is done willfully, because grace gives you the power to overcome sin. Romans 5:21 says, *"That as sin hath reigned unto death, even so might grace reign through righteousness unto eternal life by Jesus Christ our Lord."* Grace reigning means, you don't have to sin if you don't want to, because grace reigns, its in control!

WILLFUL, INTENTIONAL, HABITUAL SIN

Hebrews 10:26-31 says *"For if we sin wilfully after that we have received the knowledge of the truth, there remaineth no more sacrifice for sins, But a certain fearful looking for of judgment and fiery indignation, which shall devour the adversaries. He that despised Moses' law died without mercy under two or three witnesses: Of how much sorer punishment, suppose ye, shall he be thought worthy, who hath trodden under foot the Son of God, and hath counted the blood of the covenant, wherewith he was sanctified, an unholy thing, and hath done despite unto the Spirit of grace? For we know him that hath said, Vengeance belongeth unto me, I will recompense, saith the Lord. And again, The Lord shall judge his people. It is a fearful thing to fall into the hands of the living God."*

These verses of scripture in Hebrews show that there is a difference between sin that is committed willfully and intentionally, and sin that is committed unintentionally. The Word of God tells us that all men sin, but as we read the Bible we see that not all sin is committed intentionally or willfully. Some people commit sin willfully or deliberately and others sin, because they are deceived. I believe Adam and Eve are a great example of people who sin willfully and those whose sin is not willful, but as a result of deception or lack of knowledge.

The Bible, in 1 Timothy 2:14 says, *"And Adam was not deceived, but the woman being deceived was in the transgression."* So both of them sinned, but the woman, Eve's sin was due to deception. Adam's sin on the other hand was willful, deliberate, and intentional.

If you've ever wondered why and what caused Adam to sin, so have I. That might be the million-dollar question. I believe it was Adam's love for Eve that caused him to sin. Adam knew that God said on the day that you eat of the fruit of the tree of the knowledge of good and evil they would surely die, and so, because of his intense love for Eve he decided to eat the fruit and die with her rather than live without her. (my hypothesis)

ALL MEN SIN!

There are three places in the Bible that say, *"there is no man that sinneth not."*

1 Kings 8:46 *"If they sin against thee, (for there is no man that sinneth not,) and thou be angry with them, and deliver them to the enemy, so that they carry them away captives unto the land of the enemy, far or near."*
2 Chronicles 6:36 *"If they sin against thee, (for there is no man which sinneth not,) and thou be angry with them, and deliver them over before their enemies, and they carry them away captives unto a land far off or near."*
Ecclesiastes 7:20 *"For there is not a just man upon earth, that doeth good, and sinneth not."*
"There is no man that sinneth not," is not just talking about men in the Old Testament. I believe it's referring to men in the Old and New Testament. The question is, whether or not their acts of sin are willful and intentional, or as a result of deception or even ignorance.

There are also those who have practiced sinning for so long that it has become a habit. Once sin has become a habit, there's no longer any need for deception or coercion. It's like breathing; you do it without even thinking about it.
In the Old Testament, the punishment for unintentional sin was different than for intentional sin.

UNINTENTIONAL VS. INTENTIONAL SIN

Numbers 15:22-29, *"And if ye have erred, and not observed all these commandments, which the Lord hath spoken unto Moses, Even all that the Lord hath commanded you by the hand of Moses, from the day that the Lord commanded Moses, and henceforward among your generations; Then it shall be, if ought be committed by ignorance without the knowledge of the congregation, that all the congregation shall offer one young bullock for a burnt offering, for a sweet savour unto the Lord, with his meat offering, and his drink offering, according to the manner, and one kid of the goats for a sin offering. And the priest shall make an atonement for all the congregation of the children of Israel, and it shall be forgiven them; for it is ignorance: and they shall bring their offering, a sacrifice made by fire unto the Lord, and their sin offering before the Lord, for their ignorance: And it shall be forgiven all the congregation of*

98

the children of Israel, and the stranger that sojourneth among them; seeing all the people were in ignorance. And if any soul sin through ignorance, then he shall bring a she goat of the first year for a sin offering. And the priest shall make an atonement for the soul that sinneth ignorantly, when he sinneth by ignorance before the Lord, to make an atonement for him; and it shall be forgiven him. Ye shall have one law for him that sinneth through ignorance, both for him that is born among the children of Israel, and for the stranger that sojourneth among them."

The fact that there was a difference in the treatment for someone who committed an intentional sin and someone who committed an unintentional sin due to ignorance under the Mosaic Law shows that God has always been a God of grace.

DELIBERATE, PRESUMPTUOUS SIN

Numbers 15:30-36, *"But the soul that doeth ought presumptuously, whether he be born in the land, or a stranger, the same reproacheth the Lord; and that soul shall be cut off from among his people. Because he hath despised the word of the Lord, and hath broken his commandment, that soul shall utterly be cut off; his iniquity shall be upon him. And while the children of Israel were in the wilderness, they found a man that gathered sticks upon the sabbath day. And they that found him gathering sticks brought him unto Moses and Aaron, and unto all the congregation. And they put him in ward, because it was not declared what should be done to him. And the Lord said unto Moses, The man shall be surely put to death: all the congregation shall stone him with stones without the camp. And all the congregation brought him without the camp, and stoned him with stones, and he died; as the Lord commanded Moses."*

This is how God dealt with presumptuous sin under the law before grace. So, if you're not under the law, but under grace, does that change how God judges and punishes sin? I believe the judgment and punishment for sin under grace might be harsher and more severe, because grace empowers you to overcome sin; which means you really have no excuse whatsoever for sinning. Hebrews 10:28-29 (AMP) says, *"Anyone who has ignored and set aside the Law of Moses is put to death without mercy on the testimony of two or three witnesses. How much greater punishment do you think he will deserve who has rejected and trampled under foot the Son of God, and has considered unclean and common the blood of the covenant that sanctified him, and has insulted the Spirit of grace [who imparts the unmerited favor and blessing of God]?"*

According to this, people under grace receive **"greater punishment"** for sin than people under the Law.

The fact that there was a difference in the treatment for someone who committed an intentional sin and someone who committed an unintentional sin is evidence of the grace of God in the Old Testament. Under the Law if a person sinned the penalty was death, but when you take into consideration the person's motive when they committed the sin, then that's grace. Grace is why your motive matters.

There is a penalty for driving through a red light. In most cases you'd probably get a ticket. But if you had a legitimate reason for going through the red light, the police officer might give you a verbal warning instead; that's grace. Anytime motive is considered as a factor, that's grace.

One of the definitions of grace is preferential treatment. Not because you deserve it, earned it, or you're worthy of it, it's completely unmerited. When the law says you should get a ticket and you get a warning, that's grace; preferential treatment, underserved favor.

Revelations 2:23 says, *"And I will kill her children with death; and all the churches shall know that I am he which searcheth the reins and hearts: and I will give unto every one of you according to your works."*

Romans 8:27 says, *"And he that searcheth the hearts knoweth what is the mind of the Spirit, because he maketh intercession for the saints according to the will of God."*

God searches our hearts, because the motive for your actions play a role in determining the consequences.

NO CONDEMNATION

There are three places in the Bible where it says, *"there is no man that sinneth not."* I believe there is four major reasons that people sin. 1) People sin because they're deceived. 2) People sin as a result of giving in to temptation. 3) People sin intentionally or willfully. 4) People sin due to lack of knowledge. This reason for sin could sometimes come under the category of being deceived, because deception often happens due to a lack of knowledge.

100

Romans 8:1 says, *"There is therefore now no condemnation to them which are in Christ Jesus, who walk not after the flesh, but after the Spirit."* Unlike some ministers I don't believe this means you can continue to willfully commit sin after you are born again, because you're no longer under condemnation. Being in Christ Jesus is only the first condition for removing condemnation. The second condition, which is left out of some translations of the Bible is, that you *"walk not after the flesh, but after the Spirit."* Not walking after the flesh means that you're no longer willfully, intentionally or deliberately committing sin to satisfy the lust of the flesh. It means that you're no longer practicing sin. "There is therefore now no condemnation" does not mean that condemnation has been permanently removed forever because of grace. That's why "who walk not after the flesh, but after the Spirit" is there.

BE CONVERTED

CONVICTION IS THE EVIDENCE OF CONVERSION!!!

Conviction is the evidence of conversion and true repentance. When something or someone has been converted, it is no longer the same as it used to be.

Convert; to change (something) into a different form or properties; transmute; transform: to cause to adopt a different religion, political doctrine, opinion, etc.: to turn to another or a particular use or purpose; divert from the original or intended use: to modify (something) so as to serve a different function.

Jesus said, if you continue in His Word then you are His disciple indeed. John 8:31, *"Then said Jesus to those Jews which believed on him, If ye continue in my word, then are ye my disciples indeed."* If you've really been converted then you'll continue in His Word, and you'll be transformed. Conversion doesn't mean that you'll never sin, but rather that you no longer willfully continue to practice sinning as a way of life.

Conviction is the evidence of your conversion. Before I was saved I never felt convicted or struggled with condemnation over sin, but now that I'm saved, the Holy Spirit always convicts me of sin, and the devil always tries to bring condemnation.

In John 16:7-8 Jesus said, *"Nevertheless I tell you the truth; It is expedient for you that I go away: for if I go not away, the Comforter will not come unto you; but if I depart, I will send him unto you. And when he is come, he will reprove the world of sin, and of righteousness, and of judgment."* The word reprove is translated from the Greek word elegcho which means: to convict, refute, confute; generally with a suggestion of shame of the person convicted: to find fault correct. The Holy Spirit brings conviction to believers and unbelievers alike, but for different reasons.

In Matthew 18:3 Jesus said, *"And said, Verily I say unto you, Except ye be converted, and become as little children, ye shall not enter into the kingdom of heaven."* So, if we're not converted we can't enter into the Kingdom of Heaven. The word converted is translated from the Greek word **strepho.** It means: to turn, turn around: to turn oneself (i.e. to turn the back to one; of one who no longer cares for another): to turn oneself from ones course of conduct, i.e. to change ones mind.

102

Acts 3:19, *"Repent ye therefore, and be converted, that your sins may be blotted out, when the times of refreshing shall come from the presence of the Lord."* The word converted is translated repent in the Amplified Version for both of those verses. Acts 3:19 AMP says, *"repent [change your inner self--your old way of thinking, regret past sins] and return [to God--seek His purpose for your life]."* Matthew 18:3 (AMP) says, *"unless you repent [that is, change your inner self--your old way of thinking, live changed lives]."*

The whole idea is that you're different; you've changed. You no longer do the things you used to do, because those things were a manifestation of the sin nature that dwelled within you. If something has changed on the inside, there will be evidence of that change manifested on the outside.

Before you were converted you sinned and couldn't wait to sin again, and again, and again, and again and again, but after you were converted the Holy Spirit convicted and convinced you that what you were doing was sin. Now, you can't sin without feeling convicted. That conviction is the evidence of conversion.

James 1:12 says, *"Blessed is the man that endureth temptation: for when he is tried, he shall receive the crown of life, which the Lord hath promised to them that love him."* Conversion doesn't mean you can't be tempted. Conversion means you no longer yield to the temptation.
James 1:14-15 says, *"But every man is tempted, when he is drawn away of his own lust, and enticed. Then when lust hath conceived, it bringeth forth sin: and sin, when it is finished, bringeth forth death."* Sin brings death in the Old and New Testaments: physical, spiritual, and the second death.

Jude 1:24 says, *"Now unto him that is able to keep you from falling, and to present you faultless before the presence of his glory with exceeding joy."* God through grace can keep you from falling, and present you faultless.
Condemnation leaves you feeling as though you messed up, it's over, and there's no hope of recovery or restoration. Condemnation accuses you of doing wrong, and then proceeds to remind you of every wrong that you've ever committed. Condemnation puts you down and does everything possible to keep you down. Conviction reveals your mistake and reminds you of the grace available to be forgiven, repent, and be restored. Grace, extended through love and mercy, gives you hope, picks you up, restores you, and sets you free.

GRACE TO SERVE

I heard a preacher that I highly respect say; "it takes grace to serve God." I don't know if he realized that what he said is Biblical or if it was just his opinion, but it is Biblical.

Hebrews 12:28 says, *"Wherefore we receiving a kingdom which cannot be moved, let us have grace, whereby we may serve God acceptably with reverence and godly fear."*

Whatever God asks you to do, He gives you the grace to do it! I heard a preacher on television talking about something someone tried to do but couldn't, because God didn't give them the grace to do it. He said they couldn't, because they didn't have the grace to do it. In Romans 6:11 we're told to reckon ourselves dead to sin. In verse 12 & 13 we're told not to let sin reign in our mortal bodies, and to not yield our members as instruments of unrighteousness. I've heard many people say that it's impossible to not sin. Maybe that's the reason they believe God gives us grace to continue to sin. I happen to believe we receive both. We get grace that covers our sin, and the grace to not sin. God tells us not to sin, and then gives us the grace to overcome sin.

Today, the grace of God is spoken of like a cheesy cliché. People say, "it was just the grace of God," without actually realizing that that's exactly what it was. When someone survives an accident, accomplishes something extraordinary, or overcomes insurmountable odds they'll often say, "it was just the grace of God" not realizing that's what it was, THE GRACE OF GOD.
The Grace of God has been underestimated, underutilized, misappropriated, and most of all, misunderstood. Misappropriated in that it has been used as the ability to sin without the consequence of death; being separated from God.

God does not give grace so that we can continue to sin! God gives grace so that we can resist, overcome and conquer sin. The consequences of sin haven't changed. Sin still produces death (spiritual & physical), destruction, and defeat. Jesus came that we might have life, and have it more abundantly. That's what happens when you receive the grace of God. You go from a life of death, defeat, and destruction, to a life of abundance. The grace of God produces abundance. Look at Acts 4:33-34 (NIV). *With great power the apostles continued to testify to the resurrection of the Lord Jesus.*

And God's grace was so powerfully at work in them all that there were no needy persons among them.

CAN YOU GET MORE GRACE?

James 4:6-7, *"But he giveth more grace. Wherefore he saith, God resisteth the proud, but giveth grace unto the humble. Submit yourselves therefore to God. Resist the devil, and he will flee from you."*

1 Peter 5:5-7, *"Likewise, ye younger, submit yourselves unto the elder. Yea, all of you be subject one to another, and be clothed with humility: for God resisteth the proud, and giveth grace to the humble. Humble yourselves therefore under the mighty hand of God, that he may exalt you in due time: Casting all your care upon him; for he careth for you."*

God gives Grace to those who humble and submit themselves to Him. *"God resisteth the proud,"* is referring to people who refuse to acknowledge Him and allow Him to direct their paths, as spoken of in Proverbs 3:5-6. Not acknowledging the Lord and allow Him to direct your paths is the evidence of pride. It's as though you're saying; I have so much confidence in myself that I don't need to know God's plan and I don't need His direction. That's pride, and God resist the proud. God gives Grace to those who recognize the necessity of His direction, and are willing to humbly submit themselves under His mighty hand by acknowledging Him in ALL of their ways.

The grace of God is given to us without our ever asking. I think that's why we take it for granted, and fail to recognize and acknowledge it. If we only received grace when we asked for it, we'd recognize and value it a whole lot more. I don't believe a day has ever gone by that we didn't receive an impartation of the grace of God. From the time you wake up in the morning until you go to bed at night, the grace of God is at work in your life. Jesus received grace to endure His passion, so that He could taste death for every man. David was given grace to defeat Goliath. Gideon received grace to defeat over one hundred thirty five thousand Midianites with only three hundred men. Joseph was given grace to survive thirteen years of slavery and prison. If it had not been for the grace of God Moses might have been executed when he told

Pharaoh the Lord says let my people go. Abraham and Sarah, Zachariah and Elizabeth were given grace to conceive and have sons in their old age. Paul and the men that sailed with him to Rome were given grace to survive a severe storm and shipwreck. These are all people who feared God and were submitted to His will.

Jehoshaphat and the Children of Israel were given so much grace that they didn't even have to fight against their enemy. God fought for them, and it took them three days to collect the spoils that were left behind.

Grace is a powerful force. There is nothing that grace can't enable you to accomplish or overcome. If you have a struggle, fault, weakness, or area in your life where you're failing and just can't seem to succeed, then ask God to give you the grace to overcome. Alcoholism, pornography, addictions, and even demonic strongholds are no match for the grace of God!

I received an email from a ministry that I support, that had this line in it; **"when people understand grace, they are empowered to change."**

Humility is the key to receiving more grace. The more humble you are, the more grace you receive.

AS YOU DECREASE, GRACE INCREASES!!!

1 Peter 5:5-6 says, *"Likewise, ye younger, submit yourselves unto the elder. Yea, all of you be subject one to another, and be clothed with humility: for God resisteth the proud, and giveth grace to the humble. Humble yourselves therefore under the mighty hand of God, that he may exalt you in due time."* The word submit is translated from the Greek word hupotasso which means: to subject, put in subjection: to subject one's self, obey, be subject.

As we humble ourselves before God, we receive a greater measure of His grace. That's what happened with Apostle Paul in 2 Corinthians 12. He was given a thorn in the flesh that he might not be exalted, but because of his humility he received the grace to bear it. Paul even credits his becoming an Apostle to the grace of God. In 1 Corinthians 15:9-10, Paul wrote, *"For I am the least of the apostles, that am not meet to be called an apostle, because I persecuted the church of God. But by the grace of God I am what I am: and his grace which* was bestowed upon me was not in vain; but I laboured more abundantly than they all: yet not I, but the grace of God which was with me."

Paul says he is the least of the apostles, and not even worthy to be called an apostle. This type of humility causes the release of the grace of God that's sufficient for the task at hand.

John 3:30 (AMPC) says, *"He must increase, but I must decrease. [He must grow more prominent; I must grow less so."*

GOD HATES SIN!!!

Proverbs 6:16-19 says, *"These six things doth the Lord hate: yea, seven are an abomination unto him: A proud look, a lying tongue, and hands that shed innocent blood, An heart that deviseth wicked imaginations, feet that be swift in running to mischief, A false witness that speaketh lies, and he that soweth discord among brethren."* God hates sin!

1 John 5:17 says, *"All unrighteousness is sin: and there is a sin not unto death."* If God hates sin and all unrighteousness is sin, then I think it's also safe to say, God hates unrighteousness, because all unrighteousness is sin.

God doesn't give us Grace so that we can continue to do something that He hates. God gives us Grace so that we have the power to overcome the thing He hates, sin.

If it were possible to choose between grace to continue to sin or grace to overcome sin, I would choose grace to overcome sin. Anyone who would choose grace to continue to sin is making that choice, because they have a greater desire to fulfill the lust of the flesh than in pleasing God and doing His will. Basically, their love for self is greater than their love for God.

Ephesians 5:1 says, *"Be ye therefore followers of God, as dear children."* The word follower is also translated imitate. If I'm following or imitating God, I have to love what He loves and hate what He hates. That's what Jesus meant in Matthew 10:38-39. *"And he that taketh not his cross, and followeth after me, is not worthy of me. He that findeth his life shall lose it: and he that loseth his life for my sake shall find it."* You have to love the life that Jesus paid the price for you to have more than the life that you desire.

1 Peter 1:13-16 says, *"Wherefore gird up the loins of your mind, be sober, and hope to the end for the grace that is to be brought unto you at the revelation of Jesus Christ; As obedient children, not fashioning yourselves according to the former lusts in your ignorance: But as he which hath called you is holy, so be ye holy in all manner of conversation; Because it is written, Be ye holy; for I am holy."*

We receive grace at the revelation of Jesus Chris. That grace gives us the ability to be obedient children and live Holy lives. When God says; *"Be ye holy; for I am holy,"* it is His invitation to us to be like Him. The word holy is taken from the Greek word hagios, which means; most holy thing, a saint: sacred (physically pure morally blameless or religious ceremonially consecrated): (most) holy (one thing) saint. God is saying; be like Me, and here's the Grace to do it. It is impossible to be holy without grace, but with and by the grace of God we can do all things.

Holiness doesn't mean that you can't wear makeup or go to the movies. Holiness means that you've been set apart to do the work of God, and that you've presented your body to God as a living sacrifice, holy and acceptable unto Him. Romans 12:1 says, *"I beseech you therefore, brethren, by the mercies of God, that ye present your bodies a living sacrifice, holy, acceptable unto God, which is your reasonable service."* Grace makes it possible to be a living sacrifice. A *living sacrifice* still has feelings, lusts, and desirers, but chooses to be holy and acceptable unto God.

1 John 3:1-3, *"Behold, what manner of love the Father hath bestowed upon us, that we should be called the sons of God: therefore the world knoweth us not, because it knew him not. Beloved, now are we the sons of God, and it doth not yet appear what we shall be: but we know that, when he shall appear, we shall be like him; for we shall see him as he is. And every man that hath this hope in him purifieth himself, even as he is pure."* Purifying

yourself is not legalism. Purifying yourself is what the people who have a hope of being like Him, Jesus do.

1 John 3:4-10, "*Whosoever committeth sin transgresseth also the law: for sin is the transgression of the law. And ye know that he was manifested to take away our sins; and in him is no sin. Whosoever abideth in him sinneth not: whosoever sinneth hath not seen him, neither known him. Little children, let no man deceive you: he that doeth righteousness is righteous, even as he is righteous. He that committeth sin is of the devil; for the devil sinneth from the beginning. For this purpose the Son of God was manifested, that he might destroy the works of the devil. Whosoever is born of God doth not commit sin; for his seed remaineth in him: and he cannot sin, because he is born of God. In this the children of God are manifest, and the children of the devil: whosoever doeth not righteousness is not of God, neither he that loveth not his brother.*

"*Whosoever abideth in him sinneth not.*" This doesn't mean you can't sin, it means that you don't sin by choice! Sinneth means, sins or continues to sin. You don't continue to sin, because you're abiding in Him, the Word. As long as you choose to abide in Him, the Word, you can't sin. Abiding in the Word means your doing the Word.

He that committeth sin means; sins and continues to live a life of sinning. The word committeth is taken from the Greek word **poieo** which means; to make: to produce, construct, form, fashion, etc.: to be the authors of, the cause: to produce, bear, shoot forth, etc. Anyone who is born again, should no longer be capable of living a life that is just continually producing, fashioning, or constructing sin. Two reasons why this might be happening are; either you are not truly born again, or you haven't received the revelation and knowledge of grace that would to prevent it from happening.

Being born of God and His seed remaining in you is referring to God's Word not the Holy Spirit. God's Seed is His Word. It is the Word of God sown into our hearts that produces salvation. If His seed, the Word, remains in us, and we abide in His Word, then we can't sin.

God hates sin! Why would anyone want to keep doing something that God hates? God loved sinners enough to die for them, but he hates sin enough to allow sinners to have their part in the Lake of Fire. Revelations 21:8 says, "*But the fearful, and unbelieving, and the abominable, and murderers, and whoremongers, and sorcerers, and idolaters, and all liars, shall have their part in the lake which burneth with fire and brimstone: which is the second death.*"

Hebrews 11:6 says, *"But without faith it is impossible to please him: for he that cometh to God must believe that he is, and that he is a rewarder of them that diligently seek him."* I believe all of God's children should have a desire to please Him. Not just for the rewards and blessings, but because of all that He has done for us.

Hebrews 11:5 says, *"By faith Enoch was translated that he should not see death; and was not found, because God had translated him: for before his translation he had this testimony, that he pleased God."* God translated Enoch so that he wouldn't have to experience death. God's reason for translating him was, because he pleased him.

I believe most people are so easily deceived by erroneous teachings on grace, because pleasing God and doing His Will is not a priority for them. Their priority and focus is in pleasing themselves. False grace teachings allow them to satisfy the lust and desires of their flesh without consequence or penalty. So, when a doctrine is taught that makes provision for them to sin and please themselves, they buy into it without reservation, hesitation, or confirmation.

I pray that my life gives God pleasure every day. Jesus died for me, so I take up my cross daily, deny myself, and follow Him. Not because I have to, but because I want to. Jesus is my pearl of great price. Matthew 13:44-46 says, *"Again, the kingdom of heaven is like unto treasure hid in a field; the which when a man hath found, he hideth, and for joy thereof goeth and selleth all that he hath, and buyeth that field. Again, the kingdom of heaven is like unto a merchant man, seeking goodly pearls: Who, when he had found one pearl of great price, went and sold all that he had, and bought it."*
Is Jesus your pearl of great price? Is He the treasure that makes you willing to give up everything else to have?

When Jesus is your hidden treasure or pearl of great price, losing your salvation is not an issue that you're concerned with.

GRACE IN THE LAST DAYS

Jude 1:3-8 (KJV), *"Beloved, when I gave all diligence to write unto you of the common salvation, it was needful for me to write unto you, and exhort you that ye should earnestly contend for the faith which was once delivered unto the saints. For there are certain men crept in unawares, who were before of old ordained to this condemnation, ungodly men, <u>turning the grace of our God into lasciviousness</u>, and denying the only Lord God, and our Lord Jesus Christ. I will therefore put you in remembrance, though ye once knew this, how that the Lord, having saved the people out of the land of Egypt, afterward destroyed them that believed not. And the angels which kept not their first estate, but left their own habitation, he hath reserved in everlasting chains under darkness unto the judgment of the great day. Even as Sodom and Gomorrha, and the cities about them in like manner, giving themselves over to fornication, and going after strange flesh, are set forth for an example, suffering the vengeance of eternal fire. Likewise also these filthy dreamers defile the flesh, despise dominion, and speak evil of dignities."*

Jude 1:3-24 (AMP) *" Jude, a bond-servant of Jesus Christ, and [a]brother of [b]James, [writes this letter], To those who are the called (God's chosen ones, the elect), dearly loved by God the Father, and kept [secure and set apart] for Jesus Christ: May mercy and peace and love be multiplied to you [filling your heart with the spiritual well-being and serenity experienced by those who walk closely with God]. Beloved, while I was making every effort to write you about our common salvation, I was compelled to write to you [urgently] appealing that you fight strenuously for [the defense of] the faith which was once for all handed down to the saints [the faith that is the sum of Christian belief that was given verbally to believers]. For certain people have crept in unnoticed [just as if they were sneaking in by a side door]. <u>They are ungodly persons whose condemnation was predicted long ago, for they distort the grace of our God into decadence and immoral freedom [viewing it as an opportunity to do whatever they want]</u>, and deny and disown our only Master and Lord, Jesus Christ. Now I want to remind you, although you are fully informed once for all, that the Lord, after saving a people out of the land of Egypt, subsequently destroyed those who did not believe [who refused to trust and obey and rely on Him]. And angels who did not keep their own designated place of power, but abandoned their proper dwelling place, [these] He has kept in eternal chains under [the thick gloom of utter] darkness for*

111

the judgment of the great day, just as Sodom and Gomorrah and the adjacent cities, since they in the same way as these angels indulged in gross immoral freedom and unnatural vice and sensual perversity. They are exhibited [in plain sight] as an example in undergoing the punishment of everlasting fire. Nevertheless in the same way, these dreamers [who are dreaming that God will not punish them] also defile the body, and reject [legitimate] authority, and revile and mock angelic majesties. But even the archangel Michael, when he was disputing with the devil (Satan), and [f]arguing about the body of Moses, did not dare bring an abusive condemnation against him, but [simply] said, "The Lord rebuke you!" But these men sneer at anything which they do not understand; and whatever they do know by [mere] instinct, like unreasoning and irrational beasts—by these things they are destroyed. Woe to them! For they have gone the [defiant] way of Cain, and for profit they have run headlong into the error of Balaam, and perished in the rebellion of [mutinous] Korah. These men are hidden reefs [elements of great danger to others] in your [g]love feasts when they feast together with you without fear, looking after [only] themselves; [they are like] clouds without water, swept along by the winds; autumn trees without fruit, doubly dead, uprooted and lifeless; wild waves of the sea, flinging up their own shame like foam; wandering stars, for whom the gloom of deep darkness has been reserved forever. It was about these people that Enoch, in the seventh generation from Adam, prophesied, when he said, "Look, the Lord came with myriads of His holy ones to execute judgment upon all, and to convict all the ungodly of all the ungodly deeds they have done in an ungodly way, and of all the harsh and cruel things ungodly sinners have spoken against Him." These people are [habitual] murmurers, griping and complaining, following after their own desires [controlled by passion]; they speak arrogantly, [pretending admiration and] flattering people to gain an advantage. Keep Yourselves in the Love of God But as for you, beloved, remember the [prophetic] words spoken by the apostles of our Lord Jesus Christ. They used to say to you, "In the last days there will be scoffers, following after their own ungodly passions." These are the ones who are [agitators] causing divisions—worldly-minded [secular, unspiritual, carnal, merely sensual—unsaved], devoid of the Spirit. But you, beloved, build yourselves up on [the foundation of] your most holy faith [continually progress, rise like an edifice higher and higher], pray in the Holy Spirit, and keep yourselves in the love of God, waiting anxiously and looking forward to the mercy of our Lord Jesus Christ [which will bring you] to eternal life. And have mercy on some, who are doubting; save others, snatching them out of the fire; and on some have mercy but with fear, loathing even the clothing spotted and polluted by their shameless immoral freedom. Now to Him who is able to keep you from stumbling or falling into sin, and to present you unblemished [blameless and faultless] in the presence of His glory with triumphant joy and unspeakable delight, to the only God our Savior, through Jesus Christ our Lord, be glory, majesty, dominion, and power, before all time and now and forever. Amen."

Jude 1:4 (KJV & AMP) tells us that it was predicted that men, ungodly persons, would sneak in and distort the grace of God, turning it into lasciviousness (decadence and immoral freedom). I believe this prediction is being fulfilled right now. The distorting and perverting of the grace of God, is one of the reasons that God has assigned me to write this book

The Bible says these men would turn the grace of God into lasciviousness. Lasciviousness means; out of control, no control, no restraint.

2 Peter 2:1-3 says **"But there were false prophets also among the people, even as there shall be false teachers among you, who privily shall bring in damnable heresies, even denying the Lord that bought them, and bring upon themselves swift destruction. And many shall follow their pernicious ways; by reason of whom the way of truth shall be evil spoken of. And through covetousness shall they with feigned words make merchandise of you: whose judgment now of a long time lingereth not, and their damnation slumbereth not."**

Revelation 2:4-6 says, **"Nevertheless I have somewhat against thee, because thou hast left thy first love. Remember therefore from whence thou art fallen, and repent, and do the first works; or else I will come unto thee quickly, and will remove thy candlestick out of his place, except thou repent. But this thou hast, that thou hatest the deeds of the Nicolaitans, which I also hate."**

Revelation 2:14-16, **"But I have a few things against thee, because thou hast there them that hold the doctrine of Balaam, who taught Balac to cast a stumblingblock before the children of Israel, to eat things sacrificed unto idols, and to commit fornication. So hast thou also them that hold the doctrine of the Nicolaitans, which thing I hate. Repent; or else I will come unto thee quickly, and will fight against them with the sword of my mouth."**

Revelation 2:19-20, **"I know thy works, and charity, and service, and faith, and thy patience, and thy works; and the last to be more than the first.** Notwithstanding **I have a few things against thee, because thou sufferest that woman Jezebel, which** calleth herself a prophetess, to teach and to seduce my servants to commit fornication, and to eat things sacrificed unto idols."

I believe these verses of scripture represent what's happening in the Body of Christ today. Some commentaries say, 2 Peter 2, and Revelation 2 are talking about the same people. Revelations 2, talks about the doctrine of Balaam, the Nicolaitans, and Jezebel. They're teaching the same thing as the false prophets and false teachers in 2 Peter2. Several Bible commentaries also say that the men spoken of in the book of Jude, who crept in unawares, could be the false prophets and Jezebel in the book of Revelations.

DON'T LISTEN TO THEM

A young man visiting my church said that he was told by his pastor not to go to churches or listen to preachers who teach against sin or that you can lose your salvation. He said; that's condemnation, and condemnation is of the devil. Well, I think anyone who doesn't want people to be taught against sinning or that you can lose your salvation is working in allegiance with the devil. Sin is what allows the devil to steal, to kill and to destroy. I also believe sin will still separate you from God. The only person that wants you to sin and continue sinning is Satan! God gets absolutely nothing out of your sin, and there's no benefit to you either. Satan, on the other hand, gets everything he needs and wants when you sin and continue sinning. Jesus and Paul preached against sin, so I think I'll listen to them.

Ephesians 4:26-27 says, *"Be ye angry, and sin not: let not the sun go down upon your wrath: Neither give place to the devil."* When you sin, you give place to the devil. Paul told the Ephesians, *sin not.* So, according to some preachers, I guess we shouldn't listen to Paul either.

John 16:7-8 says, *"Nevertheless I tell you the truth; It is expedient for you that I go away: for if I go not away, the Comforter will not come unto you; but if I depart, I will send him unto you. And when he is come, he will reprove the world of sin, and of righteousness, and of judgment."* The Comforter, the Holy Spirit, reproves us of sin. The word reprove is translated from the Greek word elegcho which means: to convict, refute, generally with a suggestion of shame of the person convicted: to expose: to find fault with, correct: to call to account, show

114

one his fault, demand an explanation: to chasten, to punish. A lot of people don't seem to know the difference between condemnation and conviction. They mistake the conviction of the Holy Spirit with condemnation, and dismiss it.

Can someone be saved without first knowing that they're a sinner and that the wages of sin is death? If you shouldn't listen to preachers who preach against sin, then you probably shouldn't read the Bible as well. If I preach that stealing, lying, and fornication are sin and it makes you feel bad, am I being used of the devil. Millions of people may have been saved through the preaching of Billy Graham. He preached against sin, and it brought people to salvation and repentance. Billy Graham wouldn't be very popular amongst a lot of preachers today.

If the law changed, and it was no longer illegal to drive through a stop sign, it still might be a good idea to stop, especially if the reason for the stop sign being there hasn't changed. It might also be a good idea not to take the advice of people who encourage you not to stop at stop signs, just because it's no longer illegal.

The Law and the Commandments no longer serve the purpose of making us righteous, but they still serve as a standard of morality, protection, and instruction for a peaceful, prosperous life that pleases God.

Who should you listen to? The preacher that says you can't lose your salvation, you have eternal security, once you're saved you're always saved; or the preacher who says, God hasn't changed and He has never allowed sin in His Kingdom, before, during, or after the Law.

"WHAT HAS HAPPENED TO MY CHURCH?"

"What Has Happened To My Church;" is a question the Lord asked me. We're living in a season where there seems to be just as much sinning in the church, amongst the Body of Christ, as there is outside the church. Satan is mowing done Pastors like a landscaper on his favorite lawn mower. Pastors and preachers are falling like pins at a professional bowling tournament, and I believe it's, because we've stopped teaching the unadulterated truth of God's Word.

1 Corinthians 10:12 says, *"Wherefore let him that thinketh he standeth take heed lest he fall."* We don't teach people that they can fall, and so, they don't resist the temptation that will lead to a fall. Falling hurts. Falling destroys. Falling usually leads to some kind of

loss. It's like not trying to prevent an accident, because you have insurance.

There was a time when people went to church and got delivered from all sorts of things. Now, it seems like hardly anyone's getting delivered, because deliverance is not being taught. People are being made to feel that trying to get delivered is works, legalism, and unnecessary, because of grace. So they stay bound and addicted, and in some cases grow worse, all in the name of grace.

Ephesians 4:27 says, *"Neither give place to the devil,"* and Romans 13:14 says, *"But put ye on the Lord Jesus Christ, and make not provision for the flesh, to fulfill the lusts thereof."*
All of the false teachings on grace make provision for the flesh to fulfill its lust, and thereby give place to the devil. God wouldn't give us grace to sin and fulfill the lust of the flesh, and then command us not to make provision for the flesh. That's confusion!
In the book of Acts, when people became Christians they repented. They turned from their sin, and began living in agreement with the Word of God. Acts 2:37-38 says, *"Now when they heard this, they were pricked in their heart, and said unto Peter and to the rest of the apostles, Men and brethren, what shall we do? Then Peter said unto them, Repent, and be baptized every one of you in the name of Jesus Christ for the remission of sins, and ye shall receive the gift of the Holy Ghost."* Peter said, Repent!

Acts 2:42 says, *"And they continued stedfastly in the apostles' doctrine and fellowship, and in breaking of bread, and in prayers."*
Peter told these New Testament, New Covenant, saved by grace believers to repent, so the apostle's doctrine didn't include the teaching that they could continue to sin because of grace.

Acts 3:19-20, *"Repent ye therefore, and be converted, that your sins may be blotted out, when the times of refreshing shall come from the presence of the Lord; And he shall send Jesus Christ, which before was preached unto you."* Again, Peter, under the New Covenant, tells New Covenant, saved by grace believers to repent and be converted.

In Acts 5, Ananias and his wife Sapphira dropped dead when they lied to the Holy Ghost. This happened in the New Testament, under the New Covenant of Grace. It doesn't say they lost their salvation, but they definitely lost their lives.

116

Acts 8:22 says, *"Repent therefore of this thy wickedness, and pray God, if perhaps the thought of thine heart may be forgiven thee."*

Acts 17:30, *"And the times of this ignorance God winked at; but now commandeth all men every where to repent."* Today, a lot of preachers call repentance works and legalism, but God commands it throughout the New Testament.

Acts 26:19-20, *"Whereupon, O king Agrippa, I was not disobedient unto the heavenly vision: But shewed first unto them of Damascus, and at Jerusalem, and throughout all the coasts of Judaea, and then to the Gentiles, that they should repent and turn to God, and do works meet for repentance."*
Paul preached to King Agrippa that men should repent and turn to God, and do works meet for repentance. That doesn't sound anything like the grace message that's being taught today. God commands and desires repentance, but men explain it away with misinterpretations of the scriptures.

In 1 Corinthians 10:1-11, Paul writes that things written in the Old Testament were for our ensamples and admonition, upon which the ends of the world are come. Paul constantly admonishes us not to be idolaters or commit fornication. This is the same Paul that most people refer to as they teach about grace, and use his writings to label things legalism and works.
"Now these things were our examples, to the intent we should not lust after evil things, as they also lusted. Neither be ye idolaters, as were some of them; as it is written, The people sat down to eat and drink, and rose up to play. Neither let us commit fornication, as some of them committed, and fell in one day three and twenty thousand. Neither let us tempt Christ, as some of them also tempted, and were destroyed of serpents. Neither murmur ye, as some of them also murmured, and were destroyed of the destroyer. Now all these things happened unto them for ensamples: and they are written for our admonition, upon whom the ends of the world are come."
1 Corinthians 10:21 Paul writes, *"Ye cannot drink the cup of the Lord, and the cup of devils: ye cannot be partakers of the Lord's table, and of the table of devils."* He's basically saying, you can't have it both ways. You can't be in the Kingdom of God and continue to practice the works of the kingdom of darkness, sin. Why isn't anyone teaching that Paul wrote this?

1 Corinthians 10:21-22 (MSG) *"And you can't have it both ways, banqueting with the Master one day and slumming with demons*

117

the next. Besides, the Master won't put up with it. He wants us—all or nothing. Do you think you can get off with anything less?" This means you're fellowshipping with God one moment and then fellowshipping with demons the next as you practice sin.

2 Timothy 4:3-4 (ESV) *"For the time is coming when people will not endure sound teaching, but having itching ears they will accumulate for themselves teachers to suit their own passions, and will turn away from listening to the truth and wander off into myths."*

I believe that time has come!

STRONG DELUSION

2 Thessalonians 2:9-12, *"Even him, whose coming is after the working of Satan with all power and signs and lying wonders, And with all deceivableness of unrighteousness in them that perish; because they received not the love of the truth, that they might be saved. And for this cause God shall send them strong delusion, that they should believe a lie: That they all might be damned who believed not the truth, but had pleasure in unrighteousness."*
The reason they didn't believe the truth is, because they had pleasure in unrighteousness or pleasure in sin. Their pleasure for sin kept them from loving, receiving, and believing the truth. I believe this is why many Christians are so eagerly receiving a false teaching on grace, because it allows them to continue to have pleasure in unrighteousness, sin.
People today are being overcome with strong delusion, because of their pleasure and desire for unrighteousness. We're witnessing a fulfillment of the scriptures.

118

WHY WILL PEOPLE GO TO HELL?

Today, as I'm writing this book, some preachers are teaching that people aren't going to hell because they sin. They say, the only reason why people will go to hell is, because they didn't believe in Jesus and accept Him as savior and Lord. They say, **"Not believing in Jesus is the ONLY reason that people will go to hell."** My problem with this idea is, I haven't been able to find any scriptural basis for it, and I try to stay away from anything that I can't confirm with the Word of God.

I'm certain that no one's going to heaven without accepting Jesus as savior and Lord, but that doesn't necessarily mean we should teach that that's the only reason people will go to hell. The idea that **not believing in Jesus is the only reason that people will go to hell,** has to be based on the assumption that all of the Biblical reasons for people going to hell are related too, and resulting from, not accepting Jesus. Ultimately, I see this as just another way of saying; you can't lose your salvation, because you've accepted Jesus as savior. To say, not believing in Jesus is the only reason that anyone will go to hell, could be considered to be the same as saying; adultery, fornication, witchcraft, or murder will only cause you to go to hell if you've never accepted Jesus as savior. It's suggesting that if you've accepted Jesus, then sin no longer has any effect on your eternal destination. I think it is intended by the devil to give believers an un-Biblical sense of security about their salvation.

This idea is also a clear contradiction of Revelations 21:8, unless the sins mentioned in this verse were all committed as a result of not believing in Jesus. *"But the fearful, and unbelieving, and the abominable, and murderers, and whoremongers, and sorcerers, and idolaters, and all liars, shall have their part in the lake which burneth with fire and brimstone: which is the second death."*
This verse clearly describes several groups of people who will be in hell, and yes, maybe they're committing these sins because they didn't believe in Jesus, but we know, there are plenty of people who believe in Jesus that commit these sins as well. Maybe they're committing these sins, because they believed their sin wouldn't separate them from God, or they believed rejecting Jesus is the only reason that people will go to hell. So, is Revelations 21:8 only pertinent to the people who have rejected Jesus, or is it for everyone who commits theses sins? Is it only for sorcerers, murderers and whoremongers who have rejected Jesus, or is it for everyone? Telling someone that **not believing in Jesus is the only reason that you'll go to hell,** could

cause them to believe that they can commit adultery, murder, or even practice witchcraft, as long as they've believed and accepted Jesus at some point.

Matthew 7:21-32, is a perfect example of people who have believed on Jesus, confessed Him as Lord, and yet Jesus rejects them and tells them He never knew them. *"Not every one that saith unto me, Lord, Lord, shall enter into the kingdom of heaven; but he that doeth the will of my Father which is in heaven. Many will say to me in that day, Lord, Lord, have we not prophesied in thy name? and in thy name have cast out devils? and in thy name done many wonderful works? And then will I profess unto them, I never knew you: depart from me, ye that work iniquity."*

Jesus is telling us about a group of people who have confessed Him as Lord, prophesied, cast devils out, and done many wonderful works in His name. But in spite of all this, He professes to them, **"I never knew you: depart from me, ye that work iniquity."** Is it possible that these people were deceived into thinking that their sins didn't matter, because they had confessed Jesus as Lord? Jesus said, *"Many will say to me in that day, Lord, Lord, have we not prophesied in thy name? and in thy name have cast out devils? and in thy name done many wonderful works? And then will I profess unto them, I never knew you: depart from me, ye that work iniquity."* Are we living *"in that day"* that Jesus was speaking of? Are the doctrines of eternal security and once saved always saved a part of the reason that this will happen?

Jesus said, *"I never knew you,"* and called their works *"iniquity."* So, don't let the signs, wonders, and miracles in your ministry deceive you into thinking that you're right with God. These people were operating in the gifts of the Spirit, demonstrating authority over demons, and doing wonderful works, all while being out of fellowship with God. Even though they did these works in Jesus name, He called their works iniquity, **because their motive corrupted the fruit.** I believe God is more concerned with why you did it (motive), than what you did and what it accomplished. In Matthew 7:17 Jesus said, *"Even so every good tree bringeth forth good fruit; but a corrupt tree bringeth forth evil fruit."* The word corrupt is translated from the Greek word sapros which means: rotten, putrefied: corrupted by one and no longer fit for use, worn out: of poor quality, bad, unfit for use, worthless. It suggests that something that may have been good at one time has gone bad.
 Matthew 7:20 Jesus said, *"Wherefore by their fruits ye shall know them."* It's by their fruit, not their gifts or confession.

Romans 6:16 says, *"Know ye not, that to whom ye yield yourselves servants to obey, his servants ye are to whom ye obey; whether of sin unto death, or of obedience unto righteousness?"* Continuing to yield to the flesh and practice sin is your fruit. It is the evidence of whose servant you are. And again, sin leads to death, (*"whether of sin unto death, or of obedience unto righteousness)."* So, according to these scriptures, the evidence of your conversion is your fruit and whom you choose to serve and obey. A lot of people claim to have accepted Jesus, but the real evidence of their salvation is their fruit, as Jesus said.

If you're a serial killer, will your killing not send you to hell just because at some point in your life you accepted Jesus as savior? And what about the unprofitable servant in Matthew 25:25-30 whose fear resulted in his being cast into outer darkness, where the Bible says there will be weeping and gnashing of teeth. Outer Darkness sometimes refers to being on the outside or separated, but it was the servant's fear that caused him to end up in that place. Revelation 21:8, confirms that fear is one of the reasons that people will be cast into the lake fire.

The problem is; people make Jesus their Savior, but not their Lord! When Jesus is your Lord, His Word has supreme authority and governs everything in your life. Confessing that you believe something without having the evidence to back it up through your actions means absolutely nothing. That's what James was talking about in James 2:14,17,18,20,26.
"What doth it profit, my brethren, though a man say he hath faith, and have not works? can faith save him? Even so faith, if it hath not works, is dead, being alone. Yea, a man may say, Thou hast faith, and I have works: shew me thy faith without thy works, and I will shew thee my faith by my works. But wilt thou know, O vain man, that faith without works is dead? For as the body without the spirit is dead, so faith without works is dead also." Confession without action is like a fig tree having leaves, but no fruit.

To say **"Not believing in Jesus is the ONLY reason that people will go to hell"** may sound good, and at first may seem to have some merit, but unfortunately, I think it's vague, misleading, and dangerous. It's just more of Satan's propaganda in an ongoing attempt to deceive people and cause them to believe that they can sin, or continue to sin without being separated from God. The idea of people going to hell because they rejected Jesus is absolutely correct, but to teach that that is the only reason people will go to hell is a deceptive misrepresentation of the Truth. This false teaching is designed by Satan to make someone believe that, because they have accepted Jesus as savior, their acts of sin won't affect their spiritual well being or righteousness, and that's completely opposite to what the Bible says. Do people that believe in Jesus, and have accepted Him as savior and Lord sin? Yes! Will their willful, continual sin separate them from God? Yes! Where do the people who have been separated from God go? They go to hell.

In Matthew 25 Jesus tells of the separation of the sheep and the goats; the sheep at His right hand the goats at His left. The sheep are those who did His will and work, and the goats are those who did not. Those at His left hand are told to depart from Him into everlasting fire, prepared for the devil and his angels.

Matthew 25:31-34 *"When the Son of man shall come in his glory, and all the holy angels with him, then shall he sit upon the throne of his glory: And before him shall be gathered all nations: and he shall separate them one from another, as a shepherd divideth his sheep from the goats: And he shall set the sheep on his right hand, but the goats on the left. Then shall the King say unto them on his right hand, Come, ye blessed of my Father, inherit the kingdom prepared for you from the foundation of the world."*

Matthew 25:41&46, *"Then shall he say also unto them on the left hand, Depart from me, ye cursed, into everlasting fire, prepared for the devil and his angels. (46) "And these shall go away into everlasting punishment: but the righteous into life eternal."* Their sin was not rejecting Jesus; it was failure to minister to the needs of the **"least of these."** Did these people reject Jesus or just rebel against God? The Bible says that hell was prepared for the devil and his angels who rebelled against God. Hell is the place where all of the rebellious will go.

If you believe, the only sin that will send you to hell is the sin of rejecting Jesus as savior, then you'll have no reason to repent, and you'll be content to continue in your sins.

What about Adam and Eve, the people of Noah's day, and the people of Sodom and Gomorrah? They weren't under the law, but when they sinned, they were separated from God. Adam disobeyed, and that disobedience, sin, separated him from God. Adam was evicted from the Garden of Eden, lost the blessing, and was cursed. Ananias and Sapphira dropped dead for lying to the Holy Ghost. They accepted Jesus, were under grace not the Law, but that didn't prevent them from suffering a severe consequence as a result of their sin.

122

1 Corinthians 6:9-10 says, *"Know ye not that the unrighteous shall not inherit the kingdom of God? Be not deceived: neither fornicators, nor idolaters, nor adulterers, nor effeminate, nor abusers of themselves with mankind, Nor thieves, nor covetous, nor drunkards, nor revilers, nor extortioners, shall inherit the kingdom of God."* I believe God is talking to believers who are doing these things and yet considering themselves to be righteous. That's why He says, *"**Be not deceived.**"* We know that the unrighteous have no place in the Kingdom of God. So, the "Be not deceived," is for the believer who thinks they can continue to commit these sins and still inherit the Kingdom.

1 John 3:7-8 & 10 says, *"Little children, let no man deceive you: he that doeth righteousness is righteous, even as he is righteous. He that committeth sin is of the devil; for the devil sinneth from the beginning. For this purpose the Son of God was manifested, that he might destroy the works of the devil.* (10) *"In this the children of God are manifest, and the children of the devil: whosoever doeth not righteousness is not of God, neither he that loveth not his brother."* If you continue to willfully commit sin after you're born again, and somehow believe you're righteous, you're deceiving yourself.

Romans 6:16-23 *"Know ye not, that to whom ye yield yourselves servants to obey, his servants ye are to whom ye obey; whether of sin unto death, or of obedience unto righteousness? But God be thanked, that ye were the servants of sin, but ye have obeyed from the heart that form of doctrine which was delivered you. Being then made free from sin, ye became the servants of righteousness. I speak after the manner of men because of the infirmity of your flesh: for as ye have yielded your members servants to uncleanness and to iniquity unto iniquity; even so now yield your members servants to righteousness unto holiness. For when ye were the servants of sin, ye were free from righteousness. What fruit had ye then in those things whereof ye are now ashamed? for the end of those things is death. But now being made free from sin, and become servants to God, ye have your fruit unto holiness, and the end everlasting life. For the wages of sin is death; but the gift of God is eternal life through Jesus Christ our Lord."*

Verse 21 tells us that the end of sin is death, and verse 23 says that the wages of sin is death. Neither of these verses is specifically referring to the sin of rejecting Jesus as Savior and Lord, but rather, the sins of the flesh.

I believe most, if not all sin is committed as a result of rebellion, unbelief, lack of knowledge, and or deception. Some people sin, because they don't believe in Jesus, and others, because they've been deceived or as an act of rebellion. Either way, all sin has one ultimate conclusion which is, eternal separation from God in Hell. To say that rejecting Jesus is the only reason that people will go to hell is deceptive and dangerous.

Jesus said, "**I never knew you: depart from me, ye that work iniquity.**" Based on that, I think we need to be more concerned about *Jesus knowing us*, than whether or not we know Him. My dad used to say, "**a lot of people claim to know Jesus, but does Jesus know them.**" That's the real question!

REPENT

Mark 2:17 says, *"When Jesus heard it, he saith unto them, They that are whole have no need of the physician, but they that are sick: I came not to call the righteous, but sinners to repentance."*

Jesus said He came to call sinners to repentance. The word repentance is translated from the Greek word metanoia. It means: a change of mind, as it appears to one who repents, of a purpose he has formed or of something he has done. Jesus never told anyone it was all right to continue in their sins, but rather, He commanded them to repent (change, turn), and follow Him. Before we came to Jesus our lives were completely contrary to His Will and His Word, so following Jesus automatically causes us to turn or change from the direction that we had previously been going, and from the things that we were previously doing. You went from following the flesh to following the Word of God. Some people call that legalism; I call it common sense. Not repenting could also be considered insanity, because you're doing the same thing, but expecting a different result.

Some people believe Jesus preached repentance, because He was speaking to people who were still under the Mosaic Law, and they were. But, His purpose and goal was to introduce them to grace. The Bible says that *"grace and truth came by Jesus Christ,"* and in the Gospels we see many examples of Jesus introducing grace through the things that He taught and did.

In Mark 2:27-28 Jesus said, *"And he said unto them, The sabbath was made for man, and not man for the sabbath: Therefore the Son of man is Lord also of the sabbath."*

Jesus brought grace, but He never disrespected the law. In Matthew 5:17-19 Jesus said, *"Think not that I am come to destroy the law, or the prophets: I am not come to destroy, but to fulfil. For verily I say unto you, Till heaven and earth pass, one jot or one tittle shall in no wise pass from the law, till all be fulfilled. Whosoever therefore shall break one of these least commandments, and shall teach men so, he shall be called the least in the kingdom of heaven: but whosoever shall do and teach them, the same shall be called great in the kingdom of heaven."*

Jesus came and introduced a new way and a new covenant, but He never undermined the Law. Matthew 5:38-39 *"Ye have heard that it hath been said, An eye for an eye, and a tooth for a tooth: But I say unto you, That ye resist not evil: but whosoever shall smite thee on thy right cheek, turn to him the other also."* When Jesus said, *"Ye have heard that it hath been said, but I say unto you,"* He was taking them from the Law (that which had been said), to grace.

Act 3:19 *"Repent ye therefore, and be converted, that your sins may be blotted out, when the times of refreshing shall come from the presence of the Lord"* Repent means: to change one's mind, and converted means: to turn one's self about, turn back. So it's like saying; change your mind, and turn back to God. The AMPC Translation says, *"So repent (change your mind and purpose); turn around and return [to God], that your sins may be erased (blotted out, wiped clean), that times of refreshing (of recovering from the effects of heat, of reviving with fresh air) may come from the presence of the Lord.*

Isaiah 43:25 says, *"I, even I, am he that blotteth out thy transgressions for mine own sake, and will not remember thy sins."* The blotting out and not remembering our sin comes as a result of our repentance. God can't forget something that you continue to do, because you're still doing it. It's when you repent, change, or stop, that God can and will blot out and forget your sins.

Repentance is the evidence of conversion. If you've really been converted, then there should be a change in your life and ways. Jesus said in Matthew 7:20 *"Wherefore by their fruits ye shall know them."* So if the tree has really been converted, then it should produce a different type of fruit. Jesus also said in verse 18 *"A good tree cannot bring forth evil fruit, neither can a corrupt tree bring forth good fruit."*
The tree is made good by grace through faith. The fruit are made good by repentance and conversion.

REPENTANCE DOES NOT PRODUCE SALVATION

As I said earlier, the word repent means: to change or to turn. So, repenting (changing, turning) alone will not produce salvation. Salvation is the forgiving of your sins. It is the translation out of the kingdom of darkness and into the Kingdom of the Son of God, Jesus Christ. It is being born again-becoming a new creation in Christ, and it is being redeemed.

According to the Bible, salvation comes when you *"confess with thy mouth the Lord Jesus, and shalt believe in thy heart that God hath raised him from the dead, thou shalt be saved."* (Romans 10:9) I believe repentance happens as a result of salvation. Salvation creates a change of heart, which in turn produces a change of actions. Salvation is an inward change that produces an outward manifestation. It is impossible to have a change of heart and not have a change of deeds. A changed heart produces changed words, which in turn produce changed actions, which produce a changed life.

Mark 7:20-23 Jesus said, *"And he said, That which cometh out of the man, that defileth the man. For from within, out of the heart of men, proceed evil thoughts, adulteries, fornications, murders, Thefts, covetousness, wickedness, deceit, lasciviousness, an evil eye, blasphemy, pride, foolishness: All these evil things come from within, and defile the man."*

If you change the heart, you change the man!

Repentance does not atone for sin or produce a born again spirit. Repenting won't save you, but most people have a desire to repent after they receive salvation.

CONFESS YOUR SINS

1 John 1:7-10 says, *"But if we walk in the light, as he is in the light, we have fellowship one with another, and the blood of Jesus Christ his Son cleanseth us from all sin. If we say that we have no sin, we deceive ourselves, and the truth is not in us. If we confess our sins, he is faithful and just to forgive us our sins, and to cleanse us from all unrighteousness. If we say that we have not sinned, we make him a liar, and his word is not in us."*

The other day I heard a preacher say; after you've asked God to forgive you of your sins, and you've received Jesus as your savior and Lord, it's no longer necessary to confess the sins you commit, because God has already forgiven you of all your sins, past, present, and future. He said, "Your future sins are already forgiven."

Although I do believe that the blood of Jesus paid the price for all of your sins; past, present, and future, I do not believe that it is no longer necessary to ask God to forgive you of those sins.
1 John 1:9 says, *"If we confess our sins, he is faithful and just to forgive us our sins, and to cleanse us from all unrighteousness."* I believe this verse is speaking to the unsaved as well as to born-again believers.

1 John 1:7-8 says *"But if we walk in the light, as he is in the light, we have fellowship one with another, and the blood of Jesus Christ his Son cleanseth us from all sin. If we say that we have no sin, we deceive ourselves, and the truth is not in us."* These two verses are speaking to believers who are walking in the light with God. If we believe we have no sin or that we can't sin, because we're in the light, we deceive ourselves.
1 John 2:1-2 says, *"My little children, these things write I unto you, that ye sin not. And if any man sin, we have an advocate with the Father, Jesus Christ the righteous: And he is the propitiation for our sins: and not for ours only, but also for the sins of the whole world."*
In these verses John is admonishing born again believers not to sin, and also reminding them that if they do sin they have an advocate who pleads their case with the Father, Jesus Christ the righteous. Jesus is the eternal atoning sacrifice for our sin. Again, this verse is not being directed to unbelievers, but to believers and unbelievers. He starts by addressing the letter to "My little children," encouraging them to not sin. Then He tells them they have an advocate, Jesus Christ, which will plead their case before the Father if they sin, but not only their sins,

but also the sins of the whole world, which I believe is the unbelievers, or unsaved. John wouldn't have written this if it were impossible for believers to sin, or if that sin didn't come with some type of consequences.

1 John 2:3-6 says, *"And hereby we do know that we know him, if we keep his commandments. He that saith, I know him, and keepeth not his commandments, is a liar, and the truth is not in him. But whoso keepeth his word, in him verily is the love of God perfected: hereby know we that we are in him. He that saith he abideth in him ought himself also so to walk, even as he walked."*

Verse 3 tells us that keeping His commandments is the evidence that we know Him. John writes that if you say you know Him, but don't keep His commandments, you are a liar and the truth is not in you.

Verse 4 says, whoever keeps God's Word has the love of God perfected in him, and verse 5 says, if you're in Him then you ought to walk even as He walked, or live and conduct yourself as He lived and conducted Himself.

Confessing your sin is a sign and act of humility, and it takes humility to receive grace.

WHAT GRACE IS NOT

Grace through faith is the only way though which we can be forgiven of our sins, born again, and receive salvation. Grace through faith is the only way that God has provided for men to be saved. Sometimes I refer to grace as, **the ability to be saved**, because without it, you can't be.

I do not believe that grace enables you to continue to willfully commit sin without being separated from God. I also do not believe that grace eliminates the need to confess the sins that you commit after you're saved. I do believe however, that the grace of God empowers you to not sin, and if somehow you do sin, grace enables you to confess that sin and be forgiven. Why would God give you grace to continue to sin, when He can give you grace that will enable you to not sin? The same grace that enables you to be saved also enables you to overcome sin and remain saved.

Romans 6:1-2 says, *"What shall we say then? Shall we continue in sin, that grace may abound? God forbid. How shall we, that are dead to sin, live any longer therein?"* Paul says that we're dead to sin. I believe he's talking about the willful, continual, habitual practice of sin. Jesus is the proof that we don't have to sin after we're born again. The Bible says that He (Jesus) was in all points tempted, yet without sin. The fact that the Bible says that Jesus was tempted, proves that it was possible for him to sin. If Jesus couldn't sin, then He wasn't actually tempted. Grace does not give you the ability to do something that you're supposed to be dead to.

People believe that God gives them grace to cover their continual practice of sin, because they don't understand what grace is or what grace does. They believe it's impossible for men to not sin. Well, it may be impossible for an un-regenerated man not to sin, but a born again, Spirit filled, grace enabled man can do all things through Christ that strengthens him. Jesus is the proof that we can be tempted, yet without sin, because we have the same grace and Holy Spirit that He had.

Hebrews 4:15 says, *"but was in all points tempted like as we are, yet without sin."* Jesus was tempted in all of the same ways that we're tempted, but He didn't sin. Why? Well, it wasn't simply because He was the Son of God, but rather, because He received the Holy Ghost and was full of the grace of God. If Jesus needed grace: then how much more do you and I? The Bible says, Jesus was full of grace. John 1:14 says, *"And the Word was made flesh, and dwelt among us, (and we beheld his glory, the glory as of the only begotten of the Father,) full of grace and truth."*

There are many, many things that are impossible for us to do without God's help. Not sinning is one of them.

That's why we need and receive the Holy Ghost and the grace of God. God can and will give you the grace to do the impossible. We don't need grace to sin, we need grace to not sin.

Someone asked me if I ever sin. I answered, "yes I sin, and when I sin I receive the grace of God (unmerited, unearned, underserved favor) to be forgiven and repent of that sin. Before grace came we could be forgiven, but we couldn't truly repent. *Grace enables us to be forgiven and to repent.* Repent means: to feel such sorrow for sin or fault as to be disposed to change one's life for the better. Without grace true repentance is impossible. The word repent in Acts 3:19 is translated from the Greek word metanoeo, which means: to change ones mind: to change ones mind for the better: to think differently. Grace gives you the power to repent.

In Matthew 18:3-4 Jesus said, *"And said, Verily I say unto you, Except ye be converted, and become as little children, ye shall not enter into the kingdom of heaven. Whosoever therefore shall humble himself as this little child, the same is greatest in the kingdom of heaven."* The word **converted** is translated from the Greek word **strepho,** which means: to turn, turn around: to turn one's self (i.e. to turn the back to one): to turn one's self from one's course of conduct, i.e. to change one's mind. We receive grace to be converted, not to continue.

Romans 4:16 says, *"Therefore it is of faith, that it might be by grace; to the end the promise might be sure to all the seed; not to that only which is of the law, but to that also which is of the faith of Abraham; who is the father of us all."* Have faith and believe that you don't have to go on practicing sin, because God will give you the grace to overcome it.

Faith comes by hearing, but most people haven't heard the truth about grace. They've only believed what they've heard about grace, which in many cases has been limited, and wrong.

Romans 12:2 says, *"And be not conformed to this world: but be ye transformed by the renewing of your mind, that ye may prove what is that good, and acceptable, and perfect, will of God."* The word renewing is translated from the Greek word anakainosis, which means: a renewal, renovation, complete change for the better. So we are completely transformed (to change into another form) by the renewing of our mind. Grace is not given so that you can continue to conform to this world, but rather, so that you can be transformed.

Galatians 6:7-8 says, *"Be not deceived; God is not mocked: for whatsoever a man soweth, that shall he also reap. For he that soweth to his flesh shall of the flesh reap corruption; but he that soweth to the Spirit shall of the Spirit reap life everlasting."* Anyone who sows to his flesh, or follows and fulfills the lust of the flesh (sins) will reap corruption. The word corruption is taken from the Greek word **phthora**, and it means; destruction, perishing, eternal misery in hell, moral decay, decay that is ruin. This verse is in the New Testament, written to New Covenant believers, and it says that sowing to the flesh will produce corruption. Please don't be deceived by false teachings on grace. If you sow to the flesh you will reap corruption. The grace of God does not overturn this verse and the principle of sowing and reaping.

Romans 13:14 says, *"But put ye on the Lord Jesus Christ, and make not provision for the flesh, to fulfil the lusts thereof."*

James 1:15 says, *"Then when lust hath conceived, it bringeth forth sin: and sin, when it is finished, bringeth forth death."*

These two verses tell us that even under grace we shouldn't make provision for the flesh, and that sin still produces death. The Greek word for death here is thanatos, which means; *the death of the body, that separation (whether natural or violent) of the soul and the body by which the life on earth is ended, with the implied idea of future misery in hell.* That's why God gives us grace. Grace empowers us to overcome the flesh with its evils and lust, not to yield to the flesh, which can only reap corruption and death.

1 Kings 8:46 says, *"If they sin against thee, (for there is no man that sinneth not,) and thou be angry with them, and deliver them to the enemy, so that they carry them away captives unto the land of the enemy, far or near."*

This verse is speaking of men under the Law, before grace was given to mankind. Jesus was the first man to live a sinless life, and His life is the proof that we can live sinless lives as well. We have the same thing that kept Jesus from sinning, the Holy Ghost and grace. The secret to living a sinless life as Jesus did is: to be totally yielded to the Holy Spirit and enabled by the grace of God. The grace of God is sufficient, and it's perfected as we submit and depend on it.

The Bible clearly states that a born again, Spirit filled person is free from sin. We're no longer subject to the power of sin, and we don't have to live our lives practicing sin.

Romans 6:22-23 says, *"But now being made free from sin, and become servants to God, ye have your fruit unto holiness, and the end everlasting life. For the wages of sin is death; but the gift of God is eternal life through Jesus Christ our Lord."* Being made free from sin doesn't mean you can't sin, it means you don't sin, because you have grace and you no longer have to. The grace of God has set us free from the power of sin.

2 Peter 3:9 says, *"The Lord is not slack concerning his promise, as some men count slackness; but is longsuffering to us-ward, not willing that any should perish, but that all should come to repentance."* The Lord's Will is that all come to repentance, not for all to keep committing sin. God is longsuffering. He gives us as much time as He can to repent. Without repentance you will perish.

Grace does not change God's nature; it gives you the ability to overcome yours.

PRAYERS FOR GRACE

There is a grace (unmerited, unearned, undeserved, divine enablement) that will enable you to accomplish everything and anything in your life. No matter what it is or how difficult it may seem, there is a manifestation of the grace of God that will enable you to accomplish it. All you have to do is pray and ask God for it. Here are a few examples of prayers for grace.

• Heavenly Father, give me the GRACE to fulfill your purpose and plan for my life.
• Heavenly Father, give me the GRACE to be the husband that my wife needs me to be.
• Heavenly Father, give me the GRACE to be the wife my husband needs me to be.
• Heavenly Father, give me the GRACE to be the Priest and Spiritual leader in my home.
• Heavenly Father, give me the GRACE to be a good parent and role model to my children.
• Heavenly Father, give me the GRACE to be a Christ like example in this world to my co-workers, neighbors, friends, family members, and everyone that I may come in contact with.
• Heavenly Father, give me the GRACE to eat right and do everything I can to take care of my physical body, and contribute to my good health and wellbeing.
• Heavenly Father, give me the GRACE to walk in love.
• Heavenly Father, give me the GRACE to win souls into Your Kingdom.
• Heavenly Father, give me the GRACE to pray and study your Holy Word consistently.
• Heavenly Father, give me the GRACE to be a person of integrity.
• Heavenly Father, give me the GRACE to overcome any obstacles or opposition that may be placed in my path.
• Heavenly Father, give me the GRACE to hear and know your voice.
• Heavenly Father, give me the GRACE to obey your voice quickly, and remain committed to it.
• Heavenly Father, give me the GRACE to trust you more.
• Heavenly Father, give me the GRACE to succeed and prosper in every area of my life.
• Heavenly Father, give me the GRACE to go back to school.
• Heavenly Father, give me the GRACE to begin again.
• Heavenly Father, give me the GRACE to trust people again.
• Heavenly Father, give me the GRACE to forgive and forget.
• Heavenly Father, give me the GRACE to forgive myself.

• Heavenly father, give me the grace to overcome temptation and sin.
• Heavenly Father, give me the GRACE to never _____ again!

CONFESSION: I receive an impartation of the Manifold Grace of God, NOW! In Jesus name, Amen!!!

CONTACT INFORMATION

For more information about E. I. Osborne, Jr. and Deliverance Revival Tabernacle, or to order more of these books and other resources, please visit our website at; eiosborne.org, call our information prayer line (508) 746-4085, or write us at PO Box 3642 Plymouth, MA 02361.

NOTES

NOTES

NOTES

www.ingramcontent.com/pod-product-compliance
Lightning Source LLC
LaVergne TN
LVHW051129080426
835510LV00018B/2318